BUILDING
a LIFE-CHANGING
Small Group
MINISTRY

A Strategic Guide for
Leading Group Life in Your Church

BUILDING

a LIFE-CHANGING
Small Group
MINISTRY

BILL DONAHUE AND
RUSS ROBINSON

ZONDERVAN

Building a Life-Changing Small Group Ministry
Copyright © 2012 by Bill Donahue and Russ Robinson

This title is also available as a Zondervan ebook. Visit www.zondervan.com/ebooks.

Requests for information should be addressed to:

Zondervan, 3900 Sparks Dr. SE, Grand Rapids, Michigan 49546

Library of Congress Cataloging-in-Publication Data

Donahue, Bill, 1958–
     Building a life-changing small group ministry : a strategic guide for leading group life in your
church / Bill Donahue and Russ Robinson.
       p.   cm.
     ISBN 0-310-33126-9 (softcover)
     1. Church group work. 2. Small groups—Religious aspects—Christianity. I. Robinson, Russ.
II. Title.
BV652.2D654   2012
253'.7—dc23   2011033841

Cover design: Kirk DouPonce
Interior design: Sherri L. Hoffman

Printed in the United States of America

15 16 17 18 19 20 /DCI/ 28 27 26 25 24 23 22 21 20 19 18 17 16 15 14 13 12 11 10 9 8 7 6 5 4 3 2

CONTENTS

ACKNOWLEDGMENTS

Writers need many things beyond some good ideas and a computer. They need the creative thinking and input of other experts, the wisdom of fellow workers, the honest feedback of friends and family, and the support of a great team who will help them get their ideas into the hands of as many people as possible. We are privileged to have people in each of these categories who brought this work into being.

We are grateful for the work of Paul Engle and the Zondervan team, who are instrumental in helping us place this work in hands of church leaders worldwide. You have broadened the scope of our ministry and introduced us to many global leaders and group life zealots. We are indebted to John Raymond, Ryan Pazdur, Brian Phipps, and their teams for editing and guiding the work, and for the marketing expertise of Mark Kemink and his fellow workers.

Thanks also to the C2 Group and the fine work of Mike Seaton and his talented video crew, who brought the vision for our DVD material to life.

In the initial years of building a robust group ministry, many staff members and volunteers played a strategic role to ensure success and shape our thinking. Thanks in particular to Mark Weinert, Don Cousins, Jim Dethmer, Jon Wallace, Greg Hawkins, Brett Eastman, Marge Anderson, and others—too many to name or remember—who shaped our thinking and contributed to building a robust group life ministry.

Much of this writing is the distillation of years of consulting and teaching. Joining us in that effort were Greg Bowman and Dave Treat, who designed and delivered great training to church leaders on their own and through the Willow Creek Association. The Advanced Training Team of Bill, Russ, Greg, and Dave—assisted by a cadre of group experts from partner churches—enjoyed many adventurous years equipping church leaders around the world to build churches where life-changing groups flourish.

We are indebted to Jeff Weber, Leigh Ann Weber, and Beth Leonard for their work on the survey instrument in chapter 8. They spent countless hours creating the questions, beta-testing the instrument, reshaping the questions, and insuring the reliability of the tool. Thanks to their fine work, readers will have the opportunity to actually measure progress and identify shortcomings for the group ministry as a whole, and to do so with a high level of confidence.

The WCA Group Life Team worked for ten years to extend what we were learning about group life to the world. They provided a platform for our vision and ministry, and we are so grateful for all their work. This team includes Wendy Seidman, Stephanie Oakley, Stephanie Walsh, April Kimura-Anderson, and the publishing team of Nancy Raney, Christine Anderson, and Doug Yonamine, and Bill's very capable assistants Joan Oboyski and Cindy Martucci.

Pam Howell and Sherri Meyer brought the best of their skills in arts and production to help the WCA produce a top-notch Group Life Conference for eleven years. This platform allowed us to share ideas, envision future leaders, and encourage group life pastors around the world.

Finally, we thank Bill Hybels and Jim Mellado, who provided the opportunity for us to help lead and shape the group life movement at the WCA and the church for many fruitful years.

CHANGE IS POSSIBLE

Greg Bowman, one of our colleagues and coauthor of *Coaching Life-Changing Leaders*, was traveling across Texas several years ago. As he neared San Antonio, he spotted an unusual promotional sign for the town of Gruene (pronounced "green"). Their Chamber of Commerce clearly had a good sense of humor, because their motto proudly stated: "Gently Resisting Change Since 1872."

Many churches could post a similar slogan over their doors, use it to describe their congregational meetings, or place it in an unspoken statement of values. Leaders often blame their inability to make more progress in their churches on such resistance to change. Church leaders should stop looking for a local version of the Gruene, Texas, sign and look in the mirror. Often the leading cause of stunted growth is us; we simply haven't become skilled at managing change.

Before we plow into the essential aspects of group life in the church—how to build it, structure it, and empower people to lead it—you, as leaders, as those responsible for small group ministry in your church, must gain perspective about your present reality and the prospects of change. Some of you wonder whether you can really create a culture of community where groups flourish, people understand the role of relationships in spiritual formation, and leaders rise up to guide others in life-changing groups. Others already have groups in their churches but face numerous barriers that cause frustration and wonder whether "the groups thing" (as one pastor described it) is the right thing.

So let's address this question up front, right now. We will cover more specific aspects of leading change in chapter 9, after we outline the core issues and decisions to navigate when building group life in chapters 1–8.

A Bible professor once exhorted, "When trying to understand any passage there are three rules to follow: context, context, context!" He could have been talking about change, because the same rule applies. In order to understand the prospects of building group life in the church—whether from scratch or by expanding your existing ministry—knowing the context of your work is absolutely essential.

UNDERSTANDING THE CONTEXT OF YOUR WORK

Many of the church leadership teams with which we have consulted fail to account for the unique management context a church poses. It may sound like an oxymoron to use the terms *church* and *management* in the same sentence, but every church has an organizational context that creates barriers to and opportunities for change.

To describe what we mean, start with the following figure, a simple diagram of three overlapping circles.

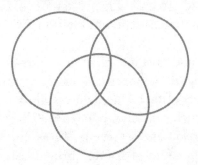

Almost every decision of significance in your church has three dimensions:

1. *Policy.* Policy encompasses vision and values, including the defining attributes of your church. Policy is relevant in any decision that sets the course for a church's ministries, planned outcomes, and essential aims. It includes the timeless and seasonal, the constant and changeable. Policy is the "compass heading" on matters of significance for any organization. Alone it is not enough, since it has to take on shape (strategy) and life (tactics).

2. *Strategy.* Strategy is all about the systems and processes that turn visions into reality. It is not the details (that is the province of tactics, the next topic); rather, it is the plan, the course of defining elements that will guide forward movement. When teams tackle strategy, they must make choices on how a sequence of stages will inevitably fulfill the dream that policy depicts. Strategy without policy becomes an end in itself, and without tactics ends up being an unexecuted plan in a drawer somewhere.

3. *Tactics.* Getting down to the details requires tactical precision so

that everyone involved knows who is doing what, when the what is supposed to happen, and how to put wheels to the strategy. Tactics involve the step-by-step implementation of the church's vision, with every step being an important element of the change process. Tactics without policy and strategy devolve into meaningless activity, but with them produce real, lasting change.

The next diagram shows how these three dimensions fit together.

As you can see, there is never a clean delineation between policy, strategy, and tactics. The overlap is desirable, though, as policy should drive strategy, strategy should frame tactics, and tactics should inform policy. Likewise, policy guides tactical execution, tactics prove strategy is on track, and strategy tests policy's relevance.

Despite the overlap, conceptual delineation of these three dimensions can be helpful. Some organizations face enormous disconnects between vision, strategic plans, and tactical performance that leaders do not understand well until they draw distinctions and examine each category separately. Leaders can gain clarity by considering how they are pursuing their aims through concrete, guiding plans and then examining how well those strategies convert into specific, sequential, exercisable steps.

Moreover, if thinking about policy, strategy, and tactics helps leaders to understand the disconnections between each category—saying one thing, but doing another—the diagnosis can be invaluable. For example, if a church values evangelism but has no strategy to engage in it, perhaps the wrong people are in charge of it, or the church has prioritized other ministries, or its leaders do not fully understand the vision. If leaders have formulated strategies to increase evangelistic activity but this has not translated into much action, they might find a lack of tactical steps, miscommunication about who is responsible to move the team forward, or overload on the system due to conflicting objectives.

While scrutiny of these dynamics is helpful for existing activities, it is truly beneficial when planning new initiatives. Leaders can easily change tactics based on existing strategies, but shifting strategy is a bigger deal.

Being aware of the interplay of policy, strategy, and tactics can aid in both planning and execution of key changes in an organization. If leaders anticipate how a new initiative will impact current strategic direction and ministry activities, they can plan change much more effectively and implement it with improved communication, processing, and monitoring. It won't make it simple, but it can remove barriers, simplify decision making, and sequence the activity shifts.

To expand this analysis, we will add one more dimension to the diagram—the specific team responsible for policy, strategy, or tactics. This will vary from church to church, but for illustrative purposes, consider the following diagram.

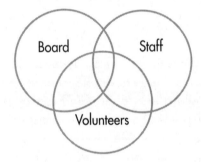

Many churches we have worked with do not know where to assign responsibility for policy, strategy, and tactics. Furthermore, the individual teams may be vague about the relationship between their actions and another team's work. They may think they should have a predominant say over someone else's sphere of responsibility.

The next figure is a combined diagram that clarifies the relationship between teams and duties.

This straightforward alignment of teams and responsibilities can reveal some of the issues congregations face. When we provide a church with such a picture, it often immediately explains the dysfunction.

Staff members debate whether the church is heading in the right direction, boards question every ministry activity, and volunteers protect their individual desires against their leaders' new ideas. We have seen staff members who demand that policy setting be their field of play and have met volunteers who do not agree with the basic values of their church. Sadly, some boards have little hands-on connection to a given ministry area yet dictate strategy and formulate implementation steps they believe will work. They never ask key volunteers who are adept at management to evaluate and help improve church performance.

Organizational dysfunction could stem from personality conflicts, underperforming players, or lack of simple follow-through. All too often the issues involve a lack of clarity about roles and duties. Clarifying the board's responsibility to set vision and values, and then delegating strategy formulation to staff, who in turn oversee tactical implementation by the volunteer teams, can release every circle to do its job best.

The organizational performance of a church improves dramatically when volunteers understand that they are commissioned to activate strategic plans, when staff provide plans for strategic implementation of church policy, and when boards stick to the business of clarifying policy and then delegating, monitoring performance, and providing accountability.

Building community requires optimal play in all three arenas—policy, strategy, and tactics—and often drives significant vision and values shifts in churches. A major shift in a church's vision for small group ministry, however, can heighten the potential for derailment over policy, strategy, or tactics. Strategic planning for any change has to be insightful and deployed with excellence. Tactical execution will make the difference between optimal relational environments and an unfulfilled dream for robust group life.

The board must buy in on policy, staff members must own and design strategy, and volunteers must work at making the vision real. If the board upholds the church's values, but then also formulates the strategy and dictates the tactics, there will be no ownership within the staff. If the staff moves forward with strategy, energized by the change in direction but without a board embracing it, and dictates the details to the volunteers who have to make it happen, both groups will have little energy for the movement.

However, what if those who desire to build community in the church work through the policy shift with the board (including the senior pastor), facilitate strategic planning with the department staff and lay leaders, and engage small group leaders and other volunteers in designing the details of how community can work best in their settings? Change, achieved in this manner, can be most successful in the end.

We expect that most of the readers of this book are part of a team hoping to transform group life in their churches. Understanding policy, strategy, and tactics, and recognizing the roles of the board (or other governing group), staff (or others with day-to-day oversight duties), and volunteers (and all who have to participate for movement to actually happen), is crucial, because you need to know what circle you can affect with your work. You live in the center of the diagram, as the following figure shows.

The three dimensions of change outlined here help to explain the nature of the change within organizations. In every situation you encounter, you must be able to recognize whether it is a policy matter, a strategic play, or a tactical performance issue. You have to decide which individual or team to involve. Does a board have to approve changes in compass heading? Will staff plan adequately to make strategic shifts? Will volunteers participate in the new initiatives? As you decide how, when, who, what, and why, play smart on the nature of the questions and consider which circle to consult.

As you read this section, perhaps it triggered a realization. Maybe this discussion explains why your church has a hard time with change, what makes decision making hard, why more time is spent complaining about what is not done than doing, how there is little understanding across the organization about how these issues work. You are not alone. Initiating a change as marked and deep as building a life-changing small group ministry provides an occasion for better leadership interplay. Your skillful engagement can change relational environments and improve how your church processes change decisions and implementation. Do not miss the opportunity to build up the church while you build community.

REALITY CHECK: THE STORY OF FIRST COMMUNITY CHURCH

Four years ago, First Community Church launched three ministry initiatives, including reviving a dormant small group ministry. They asked their Christian education director—who was already overseeing adult and children's Sunday school, an AWANA program, a handful of discipleship groups, and women's ministry—to tackle this initiative. The effort yielded eleven new groups that year but none the next.

The stagnation didn't seem to bother anyone. As long as each ministry, including the small groups department, kept its audience happy and avoided trouble, it was allowed to develop. Small groups were seen as a positive addition to the program. The church believed the small groups were on track theologically, because each used one of two curricula, both written by the associate pastor.

Last year, the church finished its new facility, doubling both sanctuary and ministry space, and increased attendance by 60 percent in six months—much more than anyone anticipated. Many newcomers, however, complain that they can't connect with the church. The existing small groups now average between fourteen and seventeen members each, and there are no new leaders in sight. The Christian education director complains of burnout from trying to keep up with sixteen leaders, as well as tending to the needs of all the other ministries—including an emerging singles ministry.

First Community's elders are tired of complaints and want to see some action. They've asked the senior pastor to work with staff and recommend solutions. The elders are divided on the small groups initiative. Some know of churches where small groups meet the needs of rapid growth while deepening attendees' discipleship. One elder, however, who has seen small groups initiatives come and go, doubts such strategies will ever work long-term at First Community. (After all, groups are not for everyone.) The senior pastor and two other staff members aren't really "into" small group ministry, mostly because they've always led traditional, program-based ministries. They affirm the effort but none is in a group.

Where should First Community begin as they strategize a new future for their small group ministry? There are numerous obstacles, issues, and potential problems. Perhaps they should analyze current tactics. They could study small groups throughout Scripture and church history or "go to school" on the most popular models other churches are using. But here's the challenge: Which issues should they assess first? How should they prioritize key problems, given the church's limited time, money, and people? Where do they begin?

EVERY CHURCH'S STORY

We'll get back to First Community Church in a few moments, but their story is not unique. Almost every church we know has a similar story, either currently or at some point along the journey toward building group life. It seems every church recognizes the need for *some* kind of structure to support *some* kind of community life in the church, and that such life involves *some* kind of small group model or approach.

And that's about as clear as some churches ever get.

It doesn't have to be that way. There is hope. We are thoroughly convinced that if First Community makes essential changes, addresses key issues, and courageously pursues some strategic next steps, the future is very bright. Not perfect—but promising.

We have been leading, building, or participating in group life for a combined sixty-five years. (Yikes, we are … ummm … how do you say … *seasoned* veterans.) Our experience includes:

- participating in various kinds of groups
- leading and coaching a variety of groups as volunteers
- being staff pastors with group life responsibility
- developing leadership training ministries for groups
- guiding a global group life movement
- leading ten national conferences
- speaking and training leaders on six continents
- consulting with pastors and leaders about group life
- working with groups and teams in the marketplace

Wow, we get tired just looking at that list! Actually, it is quite amazing. When we look at our stories and reflect on how we wound up working together, we just have to say, "Only God!" No one else would ever have tried!

BILL'S JOURNEY

Bill's first group in 1981 was a place for him to grow. He was a new believer dealing with challenging life decisions (work, graduate school, a serious relationship) and facing some of his faults and quirks. Thanks to sixteen young men and women who invited him to jump into the unknown environment of a group, he has never been the same. He also experienced a group where there was a desire to reach those who had wandered from God or who never really knew him.

It was real, exciting, stretching, sometimes awkward, but always amazing. So with all that "experience" Bill set out to lead his first group. Wow—an experience of a lifetime!

The first meeting began with four members as a core group. These were high school friends—one new believer, one borderline Christian, another more seasoned Christ-follower, and Bill. With hard work, icy determination, and strong leadership Bill grew the group in six short weeks from that small band of four people to a grand total of—are you ready for this?—one!

That's right—one. Just Bill and his Bible. He feels very qualified to write a book about "How to Turn a Small Group into a Quiet Time." What had gone wrong? Why did his three friends drop like flies from the group? What did this mean for his leadership?

Despite this failure, or should we say "learning experience," Bill hung in there and developed some skills while God did a work of grace in his life. Eventually he became pastor of group life and adult development at a local church and then moved on to Willow Creek where he threw his hat in with a team that had an inspiring, compelling vision—to build a church of groups. Eventually Russ Robinson came aboard to lead that team, helping to create "a place where no one stands alone."

Bill held various roles: leading teams, helping the church transition to a group-based approach, training leaders, creating tools for pastors and leaders, building the group life movement in the Willow Creek Association with a phenomenal team, and coaching leaders and teams around the world to build a transformational group life.

RUSS'S JOURNEY

Russ was seventeen when he was snatched up by a group (sounds like an alien abduction, but some groups can be that way). The group's leader spotted potential that nobody else could see. He not only invited him into the circle; he soon tapped him as his apprentice, infecting a reluctant leader with an unending passion for community.

The ups and downs that followed were similar to Bill's story. (Our compared notes tell us failure is more common than most admit, while success more than compensates for the disappointment.) Kids groups, serving teams, couples groups, boards and committees, men's ministry, parachurch efforts, or whatever ... Russ couldn't *not* turn each into community life.

It was still a shock the day he received the invitation to lead the Willow Creek staff team. How could a practicing attorney (yes, they always just practice, but do they ever get good at it?) have anything to offer such a talented group of experts? Hmmm. Well, God likes to use the unlikely. The resulting convergence led to a season of unparalleled group life in our church.

The momentum carried into churches around the world, with small group zealots infected by his enthusiastic advocacy for group life. Russ has trained coaches and leaders whenever doors have opened to him. Whether preaching to congregations, doing strategic planning with church leadership teams, training small group leaders, or mentoring point leaders, the story continues.

YOUR JOURNEY

This brings us to your journey—the reason you picked up this book and decided to work through it as an individual or with a team. Your journey is the most important one in this book. Most likely, your journey into group life as a church leader has many similarities with the rest of us. We'll make an educated guess and bet that the opening story (a true story with just a few minor exceptions and variations) sounded too familiar in parts. Actually, it is not unusual for someone to read this story and say, "Have you guys been to our church?!"

The answer is probably not, but there's no reason to wait; let's go there right now. Let's visit your church. We will get started by using the first of many process times and engagement tools you will find throughout the book. Each of these is designed to facilitate thinking, generate truthful dialogue, and inform strategic decisions.

Consider the opening story, a case study for those of you who read such cases in law school or business school. Read through it again if you need to and answer the following process time question.

PROCESS TIME

Identifying the Key Issues

Look back over the case study. What are the top three issues/problems First Community Church must address?

1.

2.

3.

WHERE DO WE GO FROM HERE?

You likely identified more than three issues and probably had difficulty prioritizing them. You need to address some issues of strategic importance first. Then deal with the "fires" that need to be extinguished, issues that cannot wait. They may appear as small crises but will soon become major obstacles unless addressed. We succumb to the tyranny of the urgent, neglecting long-term decisions for temporary relief.

So how do we decide what to focus upon?

It takes a strategy.

Every leader needs a framework for processing decisions and developing a plan. We created such a framework years ago after facing many obstacles and having our share of successes and failures. We discovered that the myriad of problems we identified could be clustered or grouped under some fairly clear, more global issues. These issues became the framework for building the ministry and coaching other leaders in their efforts to do likewise.

Here they are.

Identifying the Strategic Issues

1. *Ministry Clarity.* Where are you headed? Why are you going there? What does the Bible say about this? Which approach or model should be used? How do you help the congregation understand what community is and how you are building it?
2. *Point Leadership.* Who has responsibility for this ministry? What kind of person is best to lead this? What should a point leader focus on? How do you support and provide that leader with adequate resources?
3. *Unified Structure.* How will you organize the groups? How will you coach the leaders? What kind of candidates are you looking for to become coaches? Should you have paid coaches or volunteers? What structure best supports your leaders?
4. *Leadership Development.* Where will you find leaders? What kind of training do they need? Which skills are required? How will you provide ongoing support, training, and communication?
5. *Connection Strategy.* How do you guide people toward community life? What are the pathways? How do you leverage events? What about medium-sized groups? How do you follow up with people?
6. *Group Variety.* What kinds of groups should you have? How do you provide a variety of experiences and entry points for people with

different levels of spiritual maturity? Should you have Bible studies or discussion groups? What about support and recovery groups?

7. *Open Groups.* Should groups be open or closed? How do people connect to an existing group? What about multiplying groups, apprentice leadership, and launching new groups?

8. *Measuring Progress.* How do we define and assess ministry success? What are the metrics? Can growth be measured? How do we identify sticking points and opportunities?

9. *Leading Change.* How do you get people to buy in to the proposed change? What tools can you use? How do you measure the degree to which change is taking hold?

10. *Planning Focus.* How do you take all the answers from the questions above and put them together in a coherent strategic plan? Who is involved in the process? Where has your church come from, and what specific steps will have to be formulated for the dreams to become reality?

Everything Matters

Each of these issues requires attention when building group life in the local church. They each require wisdom and determination to address head on, and demand all of the leadership skills you and your teams can muster.

Here's the bad news. You have to bat 1000. You must be perfect.

Well, almost. We are very serious about this principle. If you neglect one of these areas for too long, it will rise up to bite you, and it will begin to affect the others. Stop developing leaders and you will have problems connecting people. Stop teaching the "why" of community life in the church and soon you will be managing a boring program instead of leading a life-changing ministry. You get the idea.

No, you do not have to be perfect—but you must get a hit every time, at least when it comes to diligently paying attention to all the issues, not just the ones that claw for your attention today. Such diligence is the mark of leadership: "If it is to lead, do it *diligently*" (Romans 12:8, italics added).

There are three main reasons for small group ministry leaders to work through this resource together:

1. *To assess the strengths and weaknesses of your ministry.* The first obligation of every leader is to name reality. Take a truthful, ruthless inventory of the strengths and weaknesses of community life in the church and of the existing group ministry. If there is no formal group structure, you need to look at the practice of biblical community and

ask many questions. For example, where are people loved, known, served, cared for, empowered, shepherded, and coached toward maturity? What is the relational environment like in the church?

2. *To gain insight into the causes of prominent small group ministry problems.* Naming real problems and challenges is essential—but so is discovering the underlying causes and contributing factors. You will be guided through a number of key ministry areas to assess, identifying the most pressing issues that require your leadership.

3. *To develop a strategy for addressing these problems and building successful group ministries.* By the time you are finished, you will have clarity about the nature of your ministry, a list of key areas that require your focus and energy, and a plan to address them productively as a team.

That is the goal! Roll up your sleeves and dive into chapter 1.

MINISTRY CLARITY

The Foundation for Small Group Strategy

Yogi Berra once said, "If you don't know where you're going, you might wind up someplace else."

If he were a group life pastor instead of a Major League baseball legend, he might have put it this way: "If you don't know how group life fits strategically in the church, you might wind up experiencing total chaos instead of transformational community."

Let's be thankful Yogi stuck with baseball, but if he'd actually made that statement, he'd be spot on.

Why?

Because your strategy for building groups will affect every area of ministry in your church. It will change how you lead, how you organize and hire staff, and how you craft an effective budget. What you believe about biblical community and the role of groups will impact how you think about church ministry and leadership development. It will affect how you view volunteers and how you work with them—their abilities, development, deployment into ministry, and commitment to the mission.

Everything—church oversight, scheduling, structure, facilities, training, communication, social media, technology, youth and children's ministry—will be impacted by the decisions you make regarding group life. Assuming you are successful in building a life-changing small group ministry, it will touch every person your church touches. You must know where you are going so you don't wind up someplace else.

Clarity is king. Until your senior team has a clear grasp of the role of the small group ministry, you will be mired in chaos and confusion as leaders pursue independent, often contradictory ministry goals. As a result, your program will lack cohesiveness, synergy, productivity, and joy.

KEY QUESTION

Where are we going, and why are we going there?

WHERE BEGINS WITH WHY

You need more than just clarity concerning *where* your church is headed. You have to start with answering a more essential question: Why groups? Why is community life so central?

When it comes to small groups, questions about why the ministry is being done a certain way are often tactical *and* practical. There are the usual answers. The church wants to close the back door where people leave because they can't get connected. The church wants to shepherd attendees. It believes in discipleship—which typically means additional Bible study. These are not bad things, but they also are not compelling answers.

Everything a church does is a vision-driven, values-endowed endeavor, whether or not its leaders know it. People do not give their money, time, or energy to something simply because it sounds interesting or strategically valuable. Your key parishioners invest for spiritual gains, eternal results, God-pleasing outcomes. Pointing them in a fresh direction, even if it is a wonderful one, will never be enough, at least not in the church.

You need a far deeper starting point for clarity. Something with intrinsic worth. Something that fuels passion and enduring engagement.

You must begin with *theology*. Not dry, bookish doctrine or some sort of legalistic set of rules. You begin with theology because your small group aim has to be founded on a set of theological underpinnings that connect current and future plans, efforts, and outcomes to eternal truths that trump the merely clever, creative, or functional.

DEVELOPING YOUR "THEOLOGY OF COMMUNITY"

You and your lead team can take numerous approaches in explaining *why* to your church. Your theology of community may be rooted in some themes within your history or denomination. You might study the numerous books on small groups; perhaps one of the approaches they outline will strike a chord within your leaders and congregation. A season of Bible study using the passages we outline below may also be a source of some fresh insight, which in turn provides the theological bellwether for how you build a thriving ministry.

As you formulate your unique theological framework for the ministry, it should be comprehensive, including some aspects of doctrinal truth about God, about people, and about the church. Here is one way to structure what you outline.

Telling God's Story

There is no escaping the truism that God is a community of persons—three, to be precise. This starting point signals the direction any church should go as it defines the core features of its ministry.

God always has been a community. He cannot not be one. He is, they are, experiencing this reality as you read these words. No matter when you think of God, he is not just a him, he is a them. God is both one and many, both singular and plural. Triunity (threeness and oneness) is his essence. This is his story.

Every small group dream must understand the implications of the Godhead, for one simple reason: this community of persons is the source of our relational human nature. Looking at God, we discover why *we* can't be alone for long. He ... they ... make clear how profoundly we bear this need for connection. Our fellowship with God drives us to move beyond family to friends, to push out of stale relationships into new friendships, to be defined (for good or for ill) by the company we keep. Being created in the image of God signifies we cannot escape the irreducible minimum requirement each person presents when they walk in the door of a church: they have to find community.

God has never been and will never be without community. Why would we expect something else for those who are who they are because of who he is? Community is as much a part of their story as it is God's.

But you have to tell your church family this story again and again. The Trinity is vision, direction, clarity.

Telling Our Story

As if being endowed with the divine nature from our beginning weren't enough, God implants within each person more than his thirst for community. He designed each person, and the community of persons in any setting, to function together.

In fact, for a person to be other than together likely signals aberration, soon leading to twisted mental health. It's ironic that when someone is messed up, we speak of the need to "get their act together." By this we mean that they should go away, straighten things out, and then reconnect with others. They really can't get their act *together* unless they are ... together, with others. It is how God made us.

You see this theme throughout the Bible. "As iron sharpens iron, so one person sharpens another," Proverbs 27:17 says. Translation: people will not grow unless they are interacting in a pretty intense manner with others.

You can kid yourself into thinking that another good Christian book, more gritted teeth, a better Sunday sermon, or further programs will do the trick. God knows otherwise. He created us in a manner that runs counter to our instincts. We are wired to change best, deepest, and most often when we confide in others about where God is at work and ask them for intercession, accountability, and forgiveness when we fail. This is our story.

Look at all of the "one anothers" in the Bible. The count varies, but forty or fifty times God frames up similar mandates: love one another, forgive one another, or be devoted to one another. Our stories come to life when one is with another, and in no other way. It is how God designed human beings, to form their stories in community.

Your church must tell every person in your congregation that their story is part of our story. Your theology of community has to encompass all the ways God has designed women and men, kids and students, singles and married couples—everyone and anyone—to live in constant interdependence with others in your congregation.

Telling the Church's Story

Any good theology of community will weave together God's story, our story, and the church's story, with all her global and historical splendor, reflected in your unique local expression in your culture. Community doesn't exist as a strategy. It is the essence God has in mind as he conceives of the church. When you think of your church, is community the goal you have in mind?

You must begin with the end in mind. The entire conception of the church is depicted in the deep, relational intimacy of marriage between a groom (Jesus) and bride (church). This marriage is the supreme event for which the church, your church included, is being prepared. That means each person who walks into your building is being integrated into a grand love story with the happiest ending ever written. It will be the wedding to end all weddings.

This defines the very purpose for which any local church exists: pulling people together in preparation for Christ himself. A random, ragtag, disconnected, disjointed collection of loosely affiliated acquaintances will never do when that moment comes. God is imagining a beautiful body, a loving and passionately engaged partner, and one who knows how to live forever in relationship. No wonder the standard is for the church to be without spot or blemish (Ephesians 5:27).

When you see the church from God's perspective, the unfolding of the entire story of the church makes sense. Reading the story for yourself helps to clarify your vision. You begin to see her as she was meant to be:

- Well led and structured for multigenerational, reproducing leadership (the Pastoral Epistles)
- Strengthened, equipped, and maturing (the Letters to the churches)
- Launched with a miraculous, Spirit-infused trajectory (the Acts of the Apostles)
- Built by Jesus himself to be an impenetrable fortress when stormed by the raging forces of hell (the Gospels)
- Founded on the transforming teaching and powerful ministry of prophets, kings, and priests, anointed representatives of God for a people he called and shaped as a community of love (the Old Testament)

There is no end to this story and all the ways it can be told. Tell it you must, or most of the people you lead will miss the point of where you are going, and even more *why* you are going there. If you do, your church will do for theology's sake what many will never do for strategy's sake.

When you begin a small group ministry, you first must achieve unanimity on community, with clarity — that is, agreement on why your church does groups. Regardless of your church's governance model or staffing structure, your core leaders have to be clear about direction and about theology. The slightest haziness about why you are building groups will soon become a blinding fog if you ignore it.

SHARPENING YOUR COMMUNITY FOCUS

One of the by-products of well-formulated doctrine is how it illuminates God's truth. A good systematic theology is like a road map through the ins and outs of Scripture. A theology of community will provide a fresh pair of lenses through which everyone can perceive, often for the first time, previously unseen biblical guidance into community.

Grab your Bible, put on your "community glasses," and look intensely at these foundational community passages (see appendix 1 for detailed description):

Genesis 1:24 – 28
Genesis 2:18 – 25
Genesis 6 – 9
Genesis 15 – 17

Exodus 18

Psalm 133

Proverbs 15:22; 18:24

Ecclesiastes 4:9–12

Ezekiel 34

Mark 3:14

John 17

Acts 2:41–47; 4:32–37; 6:1–7

Romans 12

1 Corinthians 12

Ephesians 2, 4

1 Peter 5:1–4

Theology matters. The Bible matters. When it comes to building biblical community and practicing godly leadership, the Scriptures mince no words. They speak with sparkling clarity to every congregation, pastor, and group leader. If you are a leader in the group life ministry you must own these texts, allowing them to sink deeply into your heart and soul.

Meditate on them; embed them in your mind; keep them on the tip of your tongue. When you talk about group life these passages should shape your words and shore up your convictions. They, and the fundamental ideas they embody, should trigger a flood of passionate, heartfelt emotion. They can never remain abstract verses and instead will be a barometer for your zeal for the vision and mission you carry for small group ministry.

LEADING WITH THEOLOGICAL VISION AND BIBLICAL VALUES

Getting your theological footing on community has practical importance in terms of small group strategy. You need to lead your congregation standing on solid ground. Allowing vision and values to guide you is far more effective than using any novel tactic, challenging goal, or clever program. Here is why.

It keeps the bar high when compromise sets in. Deciding to build a small group ministry means changing existing programs. We'll talk later about the specifics, but building an ever-expanding network of small groups might conflict with the beloved programs of key members, church traditions, entrenched events, pet projects and worship service formats, terminology, denominational mandates, staff and volunteer roles, and many other issues you don't see coming … until they become stubborn barriers.

A small group ministry done right is never merely a program. While life-changing groups may have some programmatic elements, an increased focus on community tends to shift your church away from traditional programs. A groups-based strategy is a fundamental sea change from program-centric to people-centric ministry.

When a church initiates a plan for small group ministry, regular discussions (perhaps even animated ones and occasional arguments) over how to move toward that goal ensue. The dream you formulate meets its match, and those who resist it may push you to compromise on the future you imagined.

Theology should set the standard when these barriers arise. Trinity-like oneness, the practice of biblical "one anothers," and a vision of Christ as groom awaiting his bride all bring clarity to the question, Why are these changes happening?

Tired programs with little strategic return are far less desirable than a group-based strategy, especially when viewed in light of Scripture, where community is primary, covenant is essential, companionship with God and others is nonnegotiable, leadership must be shared, relationship yields wisdom, Jesus models group life and prays for oneness, care is shared and mutual, the body is functional, and shepherding is rewarding.

If you compromise often enough, you may end up with a few more small groups, but you will never build a life-changing small group ministry. Doing that requires an uncompromising vision and set of values out of which you foster the change that glorifies God and blesses others.

It keeps your passion high when you need fresh inspiration. As you build group life, you and the people in your church will be stretched in ways you cannot imagine. The demands of small group ministry leadership call the very best out of you.

You are fighting for people's souls, and the enemy won't take that lying down. Small groups alter people's destinies, rebuild their families, and reap a harvest for the ensuing generations. The spiritual stakes are high and relentless, and there is no room for a lackadaisical effort, even for a day. Satan himself fights this change tooth and nail, which is why being sharpened by the Scriptures is so critical. They pump fresh oxygen into your spiritual lungs as you strive to reach the community summit. They provide a road map when you find yourself at the intersection of success and failure, guiding your every turn.

In order to maintain our ministry edge and energize our souls we return regularly to these passages for a fresh dose of passion. Regular meditation on these verses, especially when inevitable discouragement sets in, and talking through them with like-minded leaders, helps you to sustain your inner strength.

Reflection on the Scriptures energizes your words with a personal zeal that is infectious to those within your hearing. They will sense that you are not building the small group ministry just because you proposed it, endorse the program, or are paid to lead it. Leading with biblical values keeps your heart soft while your voice grows strong.

It keeps the plane of communication high when vision is challenged.

Those you lead — senior leaders and staff, long-term members, new-comers, old veterans, and young novices — may wonder at times why these changes are needed. What do you say? If you dabble in conjecture and opinion, the communication will degenerate into an unpersuasive standoff of competing ideas. Instead you must move the conversation to a higher plane by emphasizing the theological or biblical point in such encounters. When you do so, even those most resistant to change will begin to budge.

Never use these passages to manipulate people, making them feel as though a vote against the vision is a vote against God. Rather, engage in a loving yet passionate exposition of the Scripture, compelling your church to pursue new directions. This is always appropriate, especially when you have set your sights on a theology of community.

When people embrace change because Scripture, under the Spirit's power, has reshaped and renewed their minds, you don't win an argument — you convey a vision. As each person grasps the vision and call on the church to build a more biblical expression of communal life, you empower an army of evangelists for the movement of community in your church.

Don't settle for mere debate. Use the challenge to vision as a person-by-person mentoring opportunity. Bring them along on the journey with you and your church. Patiently and prayerfully engage them, but always from the higher plane on which you have built the small groups ministry.

It keeps the sense of need high in order to "sell" the problem. Gene Appel, one of our former colleagues, makes an insightful observation about a pattern many leaders display. Leaders are good at selling vision. Before a vision makes sense, people have to be sold on the problem the vision solves.

He points to Nehemiah as a leader who gets the sequence right. He has the vision to rebuild Jerusalem but he doesn't launch a campaign to deal with it. According to Nehemiah 2, he gathers the key leaders and laborers who need the vision, but tellingly explains, "I had not told anyone what my God had put in my heart to do for Jerusalem" (2:12).

Instead, Nehemiah shows everybody the problem. "You see the trouble we are in: Jerusalem lies in ruins," he tells them after they see, touch, and feel what has gone so horribly wrong. He sells them on the problem. Only after they fully grasp that does he then call them to the vision: "Come, let us rebuild" (2:17).

When it comes to small groups, most people have no idea what problems community solves. You have to explain that the go-it-alone strategy most people use for life is perilous for their decision making, that the only way to survive life's disasters is with the best friendships they can form ahead of time. They are never going to change what most plagues them unless they start to share their secrets and invite others to help. These are the biblically based problems God himself spotlights. You have to shine a light on these problems as much as God does.

If you do not keep the sense of need high, small groups remain an interesting option for someone's participation, but they are not life-changing small groups, the kind where people connect, care, grow, and touch others. These are only built when the problem they solve is in clear view.

PROCESS TIME

Testing the Reality of Your Theology

Take a time-out right now to examine your church's theology of community. Don't rush through the process time too quickly. Devote at least ten minutes to ponder that which reveals underlying vision and values.

You don't have to guess. There are some telltale signs indicating your current state of play. If you are analyzing this with a team or set of leaders, have each person evaluate the questions below on their own, and then use the individual analysis as a basis for discussion.

Indicator 1: How many sermons/messages have there been in your church in the last twelve months whose primary focus was community? What were they? What did they tell your church family about your understanding of group life?

continued on next page . . .

Indicator 2: Is community/small group life ...　　(Yes　　No)

included in the core strategy of the church?　　____　____
expected for church membership?　　____　____
modeled personally by the majority of staff
　　and key leaders?　　____　____
included by teaching pastor(s) in their
　　message illustrations?　　____　____

Additional comments:

DETERMINE THE ROLE OF GROUP LIFE IN THE CHURCH

There are three ways to describe the role of group life in a local church: the church *with* small groups, the church *of* small groups, and the church *is* small groups. These philosophical distinctions each describe a way that churches might approach groups as a ministry. They are not determined simply by counting how many groups a church has at any moment. Rather, each reflects the way church members view groups with respect to their posture in the overall ministry in the church. Each of these approaches has its purpose.

1. The Church *with* Small Groups

In the church *with* small groups, groups are a worthwhile, important program and members are encouraged to consider this option as a means of connecting to the church, meeting some people, and learning whatever the groups might be studying.

These churches might list the groups in a program or have an occasional announcement reminding the congregation that they exist. Or, if groups are even less a part of the overall ministry, there may be no public information or affirmation. Groups simply start and end as people form them, and there may be a small number going on at any given time.

If a church promotes such a groups ministry, provides some leadership, and there is reasonable leadership training, it might have as much as one-third of its regular adult attendance (as a benchmark for comparison) in groups. Otherwise, it is very rare for the number to exceed what is usually closer to 15–20 percent.

2. The Church *of* Small Groups

In the church *of* small groups, groups pervade every area of church life, though likely there will be a wide range of kinds and sizes of groups. This approach sees the value of biblical community as essential for every member, and everyone is encouraged to connect with others for a group experience on a regular basis.

These churches see groups as a vital vehicle for spiritual formation, and leadership development is a core practice. It is rare that people are not in some kind of group, except for the natural transitions between group experiences as groups end and begin.

With this philosophy, pastoral point leadership is necessary (usually paid staff), and the point leader is expected to allocate at least 50 percent of his or her time toward building groups. Other pastoral duties, such as teaching, overseeing other ministry areas, and tending to weddings and funerals are secondary. The church allots an intentional, significant amount of resources toward leadership development, essential staffing, training, and materials for leaders.

3. The Church *Is* Small Groups

When the church *is* small groups, groups are the fundamental expression of the church. This approach has much in common with a church *of* groups, but tends to be even more committed to small groups as the core experience for members. To not be in a group (except for transition periods) is to not be part of the church. The greater body is, in effect, subdivided into these little "churches" where evangelism, worship, baptism, teaching, prayer, and other regular church functions are practiced. Often the group leaders are referred to as "lay pastors" and expected to shepherd this little flock on a smaller, but similar, scale as the pastoral leaders shepherd the entire church.

The table on p. 34 compares and contrasts these approaches. It is exemplary, not exhaustive, but it might help bring clarity to the differences. Though there are overlaps in real life, there is a clear distinction between a church *with* groups and the other two approaches. While the others vary in intensity, they nonetheless are fully committed to group life throughout the church.

Role of Group Life

	Church *with* Groups	Church *of* Groups	Church *Is* Groups
Purpose	Help people find a place in the church	Core of church as community	Primary expression of the church
Group Membership	Not required for church membership	Required for church membership	Required for church membership
Role of Group Leaders	Mostly reactive leader	Proactive shepherd-leader	Pastoral shepherd-authority
Use of Curriculum	Chosen by leader	Recommended by staff or by leader	Designated by staff
Church Authority over Group	Low	Low	High
Church Monitoring of Groups	Low	High	High
Group-Based Evangelistic Activity	Possible	Encouraged	Expected
Models	Adult Bible fellowships	Free market, common cause, purpose driven, sermon based	Cell, G-12, house church

PROCESS TIME

Quick Check

What is our current philosophy of ministry — church *with*, *of*, or *is*?

What do we want to become over the coming years?

Organizing by Mission, Affinity, and Geography

Once you gain clarity about whether your approach to groups will be a church *with*, *of*, or *is* groups, there is another strategic consideration to address. Will you organize your groups around mission, affinity, or geography?

- *Mission.* This is often called the "serve first" strategy. Churches seek to engage people in missional activity as a first step toward connection and discipleship. The rationale is "let's get people connected to a team that is serving the community, then we can discover where they are spiritually and determine next steps." Such churches want a missional DNA ingrained in people before they settle into a formal group relationship.
- *Affinity.* In this approach, groups are organized by what people have in common. That might be based on age, gender, stage of life, common hobbies or activities, shared work schedules, or any number of factors. This strategy seeks to leverage the natural ways people already group together. It is not designed to exclude diversity but rather to embrace commonality.
- *Geography.* By focusing on the values of proximity and hospitality, geographic models seek to connect people where they live or work. Since there are shared "spaces" and easy access to one another outside of formal group meetings, there is an opportunity to enhance the group experience. The focus is often, "How can we meet neighbors, serve the local community, and provide a relational network using our homes as gathering places?"

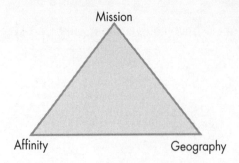

Mission

Affinity   Geography

The key is to decide what you are leading with: mission, affinity, or geography. As a ministry matures you will have all three kinds of groups, but likely promote a "primary" means of organizing them. If you organize by mission, for example, you will also likely have men's groups and student gatherings, but will lean toward mission as your primary means for starting groups.

ENGAGE SENIOR LEADERSHIP IN THE PROCESS

Leading a church of small groups is a team effort, and one that requires something of almost everybody in the church. While it is often said that the most strategic person in the life change process is the small group leader — and they are rightfully a focal point in ministry effectiveness — you will learn over time that small groups in your church will only be as good as the weakest link in the chain of leadership.

When you begin taking strategic steps toward becoming a church built on a small groups platform, conflict will break out. Senior leaders will feel that the small groups "program" isn't part of their vision for the church and people will ask why the senior pastor and board members won't participate or get behind the vision. The need: more clarity — specifically on the role each church leader is to play in group life.

The Big Idea: building a great church filled with transformational groups requires the outstanding efforts of many people. If anybody opts out or leaves it to someone else, something will break down. This could be the very point the apostle Paul is making in Ephesians 4:15 – 16. As noted briefly above, as he writes to the church at Ephesus Paul urgently pleads with them to live in unity, so much that they will embody the community life of the Trinity. Then he takes a practical turn to describe *how* that will happen.

Build unity by recognizing diversity, he says. Put all the gifts in play; put every calling and office in the church at the disposal of the Holy Spirit; defeat immaturity by moving people into service, where they can learn and grow through the ministry they are doing. Here is what will result: "speaking the truth in love, we will in all things grow up into him who is the head, that is, Christ. From him the whole body, joined and held together by every supporting ligament, grows and builds itself up in love, as each part does its work" (4:15 – 16).

"As each part does its work." In intensely practical terms, how does each part do its work to build a church of small groups? Think of it in terms of people, the real people in real positions in your church. You can identify specific names and faces for each of these roles. That is as it should be, as it must be, since there are two essential things for them to do "as each part does its work" in building a church filled with life-changing small groups.

Senior Pastor

The two things the senior pastor brings are vision and modeling.

- *Vision.* Casting the community vision means seeing it, describing it, and saying it over and over. Until the senior pastor and other teachers declare the community vision that *they embrace* with clarity, small groups may limp along, at best. Teachers and pastors must declare that community life is normal—that to live outside of biblical community is abnormal for Christ-followers because they are departing from Jesus' personal practice of group life. If they do not, the church will fight an uphill struggle to launch groups. The senior pastor needs to put the community vision in the context of the overall vision for the church, so people see how reaching seekers, discipling believers, caring for the poor, or whatever else the church is committed to fits. We will give you specific vision-casting strategies for guiding change in chapter 9.
- *Modeling.* Pastoral leaders must embrace community at a personal level. A pastor's personal journey will provide credibility as he or she calls others to community. They can model their vision for groups by telling stories, in sermons and casual conversation, about their own group, whether they lead one or choose to become a model of group participation instead of leading (which is a more compelling illustration of living in community than the senior pastor taking on yet another shepherding and initiating role). There is always an enormous correlation between what the person on the platform does and what everyone else in the church will do.

This often triggers a further question: So what if our senior pastor won't do this? There is no magic answer. But one thing is clear. The pastor will be more likely to take action if he is bitten by the community bug.

Elders/Deacons

You need two things from whatever group constitutes your ruling body (on paper or in reality): consensus and balance.

- *Consensus.* Consensus is about deciding on the core philosophy of small groups, or as we have tried to summarize it, "church *of* versus church *with*." There is not a right or wrong way, but you do need whole-church clarity on what you want groups to be. The elders, deacons, or whoever sets the spiritual and strategic policy in your church needs to decide on this core philosophy, so as you build your ministry you know what you are trying to build. When your elders agree on this and provide a model around which you can build, the blueprint you have will be invaluable.
- *Balance.* The elders need to ensure that there is proper balance between small groups and biblically functioning community. They are the ones charged to protect the church against the fanatics who will ignore evangelism, neglect the body gathered, misprioritize care, or rob missions of its fair share of resources. The church must be the whole church, a fully orbed ministry, not just pockets of good groups. Expanding community life is laudable, but its rise has to be balanced with all God has called the church to be.

Boards/Trustees

There are two intensely practical responsibilities for the overseers of finances, personnel, and other business aspects of your church: money and accountability.

- *Money.* A small group infrastructure costs money. For example, will your church follow a "lagging investment" approach to funding, or use a "pump-priming investment" method? The pump-priming technique means an investment in staff, training budgets, retreats, and the like, sort of a "build it and they will come" approach. In the lagging investment method, the motto would be "build it and then we'll support you." Even with this, there is no right and wrong, just choice. You need your board to make choices about money.
- *Accountability.* Those who provide resources expect results. Although the money spent on small groups produces many unseen outcomes, small groups are also a measurable system. A church can count the numbers of groups and leaders, and the growth in participation. There should be a benefit for the cost. Those who lead your small

group ministry should expect to account for the investment, not because of some scorekeeping technicality, but because everyone should own the stewardship choices being made.

Do not ignore the role these senior leaders play in building a life-changing small group ministry. Clarity on their role, and what goes wrong when they don't do their part, will put everybody in the congregation in play. Building a great church with great groups really is a whole-church affair.

RESEARCH AND COMPARE SMALL GROUP MODELS

Now that we have discussed developing overall ministry philosophy, organizing principles, and leadership consequences, it is helpful to look at some of the current models that align with your approach.

Ministry models are just that—models. They are not perfect descriptions of reality, but they do help leaders frame the issues and focus their decisions. Some have been around for a long time, but new models are constantly popping up, so the models we discuss in this book are not representative of everything being done in group life. All models offer varying effectiveness when adapted to specific churches. They provide examples of how churches "flesh out" the with-of-is decision.

Appendix 2 describes some popular models. Take a moment to review the models described there.

ADAPTING THE MODEL

The choices you make when building a life-changing small group ministry directly impact every subsequent decision. Beginning with theology, your process moves forward in this manner:

Theology of Community
   ➙ Role of Groups
      ➙ Engage Senior Leadership
        ➙ Model Selection
          ➙ Adapting Your Model

The goal at each stage is clarity, which enables your leadership team to remain like-minded with respect to the direction and implementation of group life. Following this process enables you to provide clear, consistent communication to the entire congregation, and the vision for group life moves forward.

A CASE STUDY

Willow Creek's "Seeker Plus Meta Model" Adaptation

Willow Creek Community Church has pioneered what is commonly referred to as a "seeker-targeted" church strategy. The label is not comprehensive in describing the church's ministry, but it does capture its evangelistic focus, particularly as it is expressed through the church's public services.

The seeker model typically features two weekly public services, one on the weekend, and one during the week. The weekend service usually embraces a seeker-targeted emphasis by its themes and its use of contemporary music forms, the arts, and biblical teaching on topics of interest to those exploring but unconvinced about Christianity.

After many years of evangelistic fruit using a seeker-targeted approach, Willow Creek made a strategic decision to structure the entire ministry with a network of groups churchwide. The church defined its theology of community and then determined the role of groups — that Willow Creek would become a church *of* small groups, so that every ministry, whether for children, students, women, men, couples, singles, care, sports, serving, or whatever, would be built through groups.

The model that best fit Willow Creek's theology and its decisions about the role of groups at the time was the metachurch model (see appendix 2 for more information on models). Leaders at Willow Creek purchased and read books, introduced new language, and started initial experiments.

Willow Creek did not, however, determine initially how these two models (meta and seeker) were supposed to fit together. Clearly, the church was not abandoning its seeker-targeted service and evangelism strategy. Two weekly services continued. Meanwhile, the church identified and trained small group leaders, launched new groups, and connected an increasing number of people to groups.

When some small groups began to suggest that they would now pursue evangelism through their group — a concept included in the metachurch small group model — they also concluded doing so would allow them to skip participation in the weekend seeker service. The meta and seeker models collided.

Willow Creek soon discovered another step in the process of reaching clarity about small groups. The perception of "having groups *versus* weekend services" needed to be replaced by the reality of "groups *plus* weekends." The metachurch model had to be adapted to fit other defining features of the church's overall ministry and congregation. Everything about meta would not fit Willow Creek perfectly. "Seeker plus meta" meant merging an evangelistic model with a connection and discipleship process.

Adapting a model means discerning how to tailor a given small group model to your setting. In the process you must discover what works best for your church (again, there is no right or wrong way to build community with groups). Choosing a model is the starting point, because it provides a set of common ideas and a language that allows you to implement change more quickly. Having clarity about your approach will allow you to adapt a model to fit your desired outcomes.

Here's a list of strategic questions designed to assist you in the decision-making process.

1. What are the one or two hallmarks of your church that must remain a part of its life after you establish a small group ministry? Perhaps your church has been as evangelistic as Willow Creek. Maybe compassion and justice are nonnegotiable, or ministry to children has been the key to reaching families in your community. It might be a foreign missions focus, your Christian school, or intensive internal parish programs. What essential strategy has to be merged with a future shift to small groups?

2. Imagine what your church will look like a year or two after the successful launch of the small groups model. What core mission will naturally collide with future group life? What will tend to force people to choose one over the other? How should group strategies be tailored now to anticipate those conflicts?

3. On the positive side, how can you leverage the existing ministry focus to enhance the community/group life initiative? Similarly, how can the small group model you've selected be tailored to benefit the church's existing mission?

4. How will you communicate clearly to your church the plans for integrating what has mattered most in the past when you introduce the new group life initiative? What will be confusing about what is in place already when you start the new community model?

5. Who will negotiate the pinch points? Who believes strongly in *both* models and can therefore sufficiently confer about adaptation? When confusion sets in and resources must be allocated, conflicts resolved, and the like, who has sufficient understanding of all sides of the issues to help the senior leadership navigate the integration?

You will know that the adaptation process is working well when people in your church start to refer to the small group ministry as "The [Your Church Name] model." It happened at Willow Creek, where people eventually ignored any reference to the meta model, and called it "the Willow small group model." The reference implied that the adaptation had been effective.

ALIGNING YOUR MINISTRIES TO YOUR MODEL

Remember the word we started with: *clarity*. The purpose of focusing on theology is to be sure everyone clearly understands your small group ministry's direction and purpose. Defining the role of groups brings clarity to your assumptions about what groups mean to church life. Model selection makes strategy and language clearer. Adapting is an exercise in clarifying other critical aspects of your church focus and how the group initiative will integrate with it. However, there is one more clarity step. It flows as before like this:

> **Theology of Community**
> → Role of Groups
> → Engage Senior Leadership
> → Model Selection
> → Adapting Your Model
> → Aligning Your Ministries

How all of your ministries align to your vision and model for group life is *the* test of whether you've achieved clarity. Addressing alignment affects every aspect of congregational life.

Here is why: most ministries in a church are led by either staff or volunteers who think of their ministry like a store in a shopping center. They are glad for the space in the mall, but focus solely on their own business, remaining aware of other shops only to the extent they must. They cooperate with the shopping center when it benefits them. This perspective doesn't make them bad people. It is a mindset that develops out of positive passion for their calling, expertise to meet the needs they do, and investment made in building their ministry.

If you seek to become a "church of groups," however, you need to move from the shopping mall to the department store. Ministries within a department store–style church have a higher level of integration into the vision and strategy underlying the small group effort. When ministries within a church view themselves in this way, the language used to describe roles and tactics becomes unified across departments. The methods of organization used for small groups translate into each subministry so they function more similarly. Each area, as a part of a larger whole, has to increase their interest in how other parts of the store are doing.

The positive steps required to move from shopping mall to department store involve *alignment*. Alignment means analyzing each ministry and its approach to meeting needs. For example, how will small groups work for elementary age children versus high school students? Couples and singles? Men and women? Church leaders can apply a similar organizational approach across ministries, but how groups are formed, what their objectives are, and when and where they meet will diverge.

The terms used to refer to leadership roles and to describe how congregants move from gatherings to groups have become common. Some training strategies involve the whole church, while other, department-specific efforts may apply the broader lessons to the interests of a particular area. For example, many small group leaders must do the same things whether working with care groups or serving groups, but there are unique aspects groups in those areas have to deal with. Alignment across ministries requires the joint efforts of both centralized small group leadership and decentralized department heads.

Comprehensive alignment will move in two directions, vertical and horizontal.

Vertical Alignment

Vertical alignment means focus on a common goal. Consider the Willow Creek case study. Adapting the metachurch model required integrating small groups and whole-church evangelism. Aligning ministries to the adapted groups strategy demanded not only the department-by-department work described above. Beyond that, all ministries of the church benefited when leaders identified common goals. In the case of Willow Creek, there were two goals — a *quantitative* goal and a *qualitative* goal.

The ten-year quantitative goal was to connect twenty thousand individuals into small groups. This figure was not an end in itself. It signaled something far greater, that the church had become a church of groups, a place where everyone who wanted a group was connected. It meant giving every person attending the church a clear pathway to a John 17 experience. There would be a place for every woman, man, single, couple, student, and child.

Since there were approximately fifteen subministries, the common quantitative goal could be broken down to each ministry on a department and annual basis. Within a ministry, then, each leader could engage in the progress toward the whole-church goal. It wasn't about the number; it was about getting everyone connected in a life-changing group.

The qualitative goal was a by-product of the church's common spiritual development framework at that time, popularly known as "the five Gs."

The framework answered the simple question of what increasing maturity looks like. The five Gs call for progress in each of these areas:

1. Grace: evangelistic fruit
2. Growth: character transformation
3. Groups: life-changing relationships
4. Gifts: joyful service
5. Good Stewardship: generous giving

Based on the common understanding of the life change to be reproduced in each individual, which could be adapted to each ministry, the qualitative goal for groups could follow naturally from the goal for individuals. Connecting twenty thousand people into "five G groups"—small communities designed to move each person forward in the five Gs—could express the quantitative and qualitative goal every leader in every ministry could own, together.

Having a common goal produces vertical alignment—every ministry of the church working toward churchwide objectives and mission. Thus each part becomes more vital, since every aspect of the ministry must function at its best for the other dimensions of the church to be optimized. Ministries to families will only be as good as the ministry to parents and to children. Singles, once married, need the couples ministry to be effective. People in crisis need the care ministries to be effective.

With a common groups approach, parents can talk with their kids about church using a common language and structure. Individuals can move from one kind of group to another without having to reorient to how the ministry operates.

The result: horizontal alignment.

Horizontal Alignment

Horizontal alignment means working together to reach the goal. Without common goals, ministries within most churches tend to become independently functioning silos. Vertical alignment breaks down those silos and opens up the potential for departments to do something even more powerful *together*.

Shared language and structure fosters horizontal alignment. Leaders can move from one department to another without having to relearn strategy. As children progress from elementary to middle school to high school, the common experience of group life fosters both continuity and momentum.

In addition, leaders of each ministry can identify opportunities to pursue initiatives that will not only benefit their department, but grow other ministries. An outreach to children can be planned in ways that will help their parents. Care ministries can meet people in need, designing support or care groups that will lead to a cleaner handoff to men's groups and women's groups ready to receive them when they are through the season of care. Evangelistic groups can help transition new Christians into new life in Christ, and serving groups can allow unconnected people to experiment with their first connections into community and then help transition them into more intensive discipleship groups in due course.

It is a bit of an oversimplification, but alignment, horizontal alignment in particular, can be thought of as an equation:

Alignment = Communication + Coordination + Collaboration

Assume your church is going to host a Friday night outreach party for your children's ministry. Each of your fifth graders is bringing two or three of their friends with no church connection. Skillful planning, effective communication, fun programming, and an unexpectedly high response make the event a raving success.

Unfortunately, due to a "ministry silo" dynamic, a key problem develops. Since most of the church's facilities are needed for the children's ministry event, adult ministries with smaller gatherings that same night become extremely frustrated by the numerous distractions. They know Jesus said, "Suffer the little children to come unto me," but now they envision the verse as "Bring suffering to the little children"—an entirely different meaning.

This illustration is a prime example for beginning the alignment discussions. How does it work in this situation?

- *Communication.* Gather key ministry leaders together regularly and discuss calendars, facility use, budgets, annual rhythms for events, and the like. Connect key leaders (a sort of "ministry board of directors") who embrace the mission of making the entire church thrive (not just their silo). You need them to effectively run their ministry *and* foster the movement of your whole congregation toward group life.
- *Coordination.* As ministries improve cross-department communication, it opens the door to better coordination. When does it make sense to dedicate all facilities for one ministry's gain? How should weekly event rhythms be shifted to optimize what serves a particular ministry best? What if weekly platform announcements and program inserts highlighted one or two key happenings all the ministries are cheering for, instead of the overstuffed bulletin and blur of rapidly referenced calendars obscuring what matters? Where are training

processes redundant, so some efficiency could be gained by coordinating all ministries' leadership development?

- *Collaboration.* A common small group model and future ministry development focus supply one further addition to the alignment equation. With the children's ministry event discussed above, *collaboration* would have produced a novel thought among that department's leaders: what if we talked to the couples' ministry about how they could leverage what we're doing? Parents are driving to the church campus anyway, so it could be a prime opportunity to host a parenting seminar out of which the couples' ministry could launch parenting small groups. Let's collaborate!

Once your church takes alignment seriously, you will be astonished to see how many ministry opportunities there are when departments communicate, coordinate, and collaborate. Alignment offers numerous ways to make not only incremental, but also exponential, gains in efficiency, strategic payoff, and mutual support.

PROCESS TIME

Next Steps for Your Ministry

Your reading of this handbook is only as valuable as the analysis you do after completing each section. Analysis is not just a reflection exercise, though. It requires formulating some initial thoughts about what to do in response to what you discern.

Before you begin, make note of recurring phrases "next steps" and "what steps?" in the text below. Your process will only be as good as the action steps you begin to brainstorm now. You do not need to commit to them just yet, since future process times will pull together the sequence of evaluation and planning.

As noted in the previous process time, if you are working through this study with others, allow sufficient time for everyone involved to formulate independent thoughts, and then use the conclusions to foster discussion and joint planning.

First, determine your church's top need:

	Yes	No
Community is a *core value*, embedded in our church's vision and practices.	—	—
The *role* small groups will play in building community in our church is clear.	—	—

We have chosen a *model* and are adapting it
   to our culture.
All of our ministries are in *alignment* to our model.   ___   ___
Our *senior leaders* are clear on and contributing
   to our progress.   ___   ___

Second, decide some next steps in one key area of need. Your beginning point is the first "no" answer in the above checklist, since lack of clarity earlier in the sequence will result in later confusion. If you are working with a team, you may be able to determine next steps for two key areas in the sequence. The questions that follow will guide your planning for each point.

- *Core Value.* What steps can you take to clarify and more deeply embed the theology of community in your senior leadership? In your small group infrastructure? In your church?
- *Role.* What are the strengths and weaknesses of the role you have chosen for groups (with, of, is)? What steps can you take to deal with the weaknesses? If you are in transition between roles, what are your next steps in the transition?
- *Model.* How well does the model you have selected fit your church culture? Where is it working? Not working? What steps need to be taken to adapt/change the model?
- *Senior Leaders.* What is the church missing from its senior pastor, elder/deacons, or board/trustees? If you had to grade each category of leadership on the two contributions they must make to a small group ministry (outlined above), how are they doing with their duties? What conversations need to be initiated to improve those deliverables?
- *Alignment.* Where are you in the process of ministry alignment (especially communication, coordination, collaboration)? What steps can be taken to move forward? What ministries are making progress toward collaboration that could be used as examples of alignment done well?

Chapter 2

POINT LEADERSHIP

The Architect of Ministry Development

KEY QUESTION

Who will lead
this movement
in the church?

Assume for a moment that your church is populated by an increasing number of empty nesters, who are traveling more frequently on weekends, preparing for retirement, visiting grandchildren in other towns, and decreasing their involvement in the ministries. Weekend attendance has been shrinking for two years. Donations are declining. Leaders are taking more breaks, and eventually resigning. An emerging trend is clear: your church is going to fade over time if you do not face this stark future.

However, your church is located near several neighborhoods—established ones where retirees are selling their homes to young families and others that are under construction to attract new home buyers. Just beyond those housing developments are a mix of townhomes, condos, and mid-scale apartments, all with higher than average numbers of preschool and early elementary age children. A new school is under construction within a mile of your campus due to the increased student population.

The need for a strategic shift seems obvious. A heightened focus on ministries to children and families could well turn the tide on both declining attendance and untapped opportunity.

Identifying this issue exposes a problem, though. All of those ministries have been barely adequate for many years. The handful of reluctant volunteers who have led them are tired and somewhat resistant to new experiments in "their" departments. Their ideas are tradition-bound and tired, and the time they are willing to devote to the effort is shrinking.

Your top leaders agree. The new course toward making children a primary focus of your church has to be charted. Budgets have been retooled to free up significant funding for the next two or three years for the initiative. It is up to you to determine how to allocate the monies.

What is the first decision you make? Without a champion for the new initiative, the dreams of a revitalized, effective, and growing church family will die on the vine. Your church has to invest in the future, in the form of a suitable leader who can recruit and train new volunteers, introduce the plans for turning vision into reality, and embody the commitment to kids and their families.

Any new initiative to which a church commits requires fresh, energetic leadership if it is going to happen. Since so many churches regard children's ministry, worship, youth groups, and the like as routine, staffing and budgets are a priority. The idea of small group ministry as integral to the local church is relatively novel. It is not uncommon for churches to reformulate their theology and strategy for groups, only to fail to allocate the needed funds, leadership, and related support it will take to make the change more than good intentions. When it comes to small group ministry, the return will be in proportion to the investment.

The second critical step in building a life-changing small group ministry is to establish the role of a small group ministry point leader and identify the right person to tackle the job. We would not necessarily mandate that it must be a paid staff position—although there will be a correlation between the investment and payoff—but every church making a significant shift toward small groups will require a topflight player to "ride point" on the movement it envisions.

Doing so will require selecting the right individual, positioning them for success, and having them do the right things. Having the right leader doesn't mean other leaders (the senior pastor, teachers, and ministry heads) won't be needed. Depending on how the role is filled, where it fits within your team, and what it is intended to accomplish, senior leaders will have their part to play, and the kinds of decisions discussed near the end of this chapter will aid those dynamics.

SELECTING THE RIGHT POINT LEADER

The point leader for small group ministry may perform one of the toughest jobs in the church. Small group point leaders aren't churned out by the seminaries. The position is still under development across many churches and there's not a vast pool of veteran small group champions looking for employment.

It is nearly as intimidating for those exploring these jobs. After all, Jesus and his disciples provide the template for a small group done right. Although it can be fun to run the experiments required to build the ministry, the occasional laboratory mishaps can lead to painful explosions. The point leader has to withstand high scrutiny.

By the time you review the qualifications outlined below, you might conclude that Jesus is the only one who could fit the job description. However, do not take this discussion as a definitive punch list. It is a composite picture taken from the decade or so that has transpired since many churches have committed to building life-changing small group ministries. No one person has the makeup to the full extent we describe.

However, there will be correspondence between the qualifications below and the effectiveness of the point leader. Some critical qualities are needed to provide point leadership to the small group movement in your church.

Spiritual Gifts

Biblical leadership begins with spiritual gifts. The Bible makes clear how much giftedness matters in passages such as Romans 12, 1 Corinthians 12, and Ephesians 4. The spiritual gifts of the point leader are essential for effectiveness. Each church must recruit a small groups champion that will optimize the development of the ministry.

There are two sets of spiritual gifts to consider, one primary, and another secondary. The primary gifts are nearly mandatory, and the secondary gifts helpful.

Primary

There are two lead gifts that will turbocharge effectiveness if present in the point leader, and will slow progress of the initiative if missing or weak.

Leadership

This is the Romans 12:8 attribute, which describes a divinely granted *capability to motivate and mobilize individuals and groups for purposes God has in mind for them*. It is given to those who will assist the church in fulfilling its potential.

It is not hard to see why the leadership gift is so critical for the small groups point person. This person is the leader of a growing band of those committed to leading groups, who need to have a sense that someone is in front of them in their efforts—someone who will see the horizon and is guiding everyone on how to reach their aims; someone who can cast the vision in a way that will rouse commitment, embody the church's values so that efforts remain biblically inspired, and craft the strategic adjustments that will command respect and confidence. The gift will be used in service to the church and its goals.

Administration

Contrary to what most people think when they hear this term, the scriptural concept of administration has nothing to do with to-do lists, task orientation, and tidy organization. Those are attributes attendant to the gift of helps. The gift of administration could be better termed, in modern parlance, "management." It is the *ability to create systems and processes to turn vision into reality on a consistent basis.*

The gift of administration is essential for the small groups champion because of the nature of the ministry. The requirements of structuring small group ministry, making tactical decisions, and organizing the support systems demand something more than just a leadership gift. When a gifted leader can exercise great management capabilities, small group ministry will flourish, season after season, as an expanding network of communities that meets needs, develops disciples, and strengthens the fabric of relationships within the church. Everybody gets the benefit of a strong infrastructure, so their efforts become easier due to how it all fits together.

These two primary gifts, when knitted together in the small group point leader, are a potent combination. The leadership gift without the administration gift can result in unfulfilled vision, but administration without leadership can weigh down the church with well-intentioned processes that fail to engage the heart. Together, these two gifts will produce both the hard edge of great organization and the soft side of a shepherding touch.

In addition to leadership and administration, a point leader may have a third, complementary gift that will make his or her efforts all the more effective. The gifts listed below are among the secondary gifts.

Secondary

- *Discernment.* Much of the small group point leader's job is to read the winds of the Spirit as he moves among the congregation. In particular, the identification and placement of people in groups, leaders in coaching and small group shepherding roles, and support teams in position requires an extraordinary demand for discerning the gifts, motives, and potential of many individuals.
- *Wisdom.* Building a life-changing small group ministry requires someone to make thousands of decisions, strategic decisions that will shape the church's future. People choices (about group participation and leadership roles) will develop people's potential and multiply personal impact. Tactical improvements will demand wise analysis and judicious conclusions. The prudence that this gift produces will enable the leader to apply leadership capabilities and management skill with a deft touch.
- *Teaching.* Someone will need to be a consistent voice of small group ministry, and the point leader who can teach will add to its potential progress. If the point person can cast vision well from the church's platform and ensure that efforts to develop small groups are biblically

motivated, groups will grow into a soundly informed collection of communities.

- *Shepherding.* This secondary gift can be helpful for obvious reasons, since groups can be such a force for providing care. However, many churches make the mistake of tapping their best shepherd as head of the ministry, only to find that what works in personal and group settings is ill suited to guiding a whole ministry. Being the point leader requires leadership, management, and other skills fitted to whole-enterprise growth. The good shepherd can be overwhelmed by those demands.

These secondary gifts can also be supplied to the point leader through a well-configured team consisting of key volunteers, the small group champion's peers, or the senior pastor, teachers, and core leaders. There will be few other ministries in which the church will live out the reality of what the Bible teaches about spiritual gifts—that they are given "so that the body of Christ may be built up." Spiritual gifts have to be the starting point for selecting and deploying the point leader and the team that will move the church forward with small groups.

PROCESS TIME

Spiritual Gifts of the Point Leader

Using the following chart, consider the spiritual gifting of your current point leader or the leader you are considering for the role. Based on your interaction and observation, where would you place them on the strength–weakness continuum? If several people are performing your evaluation, separately record each person's preliminary conclusions, and then pull together the collective insights from everyone. Include the point person's self-assessment if and as appropriate. If you discuss the results of the findings with the point leader, remember the encouragement of Ephesians 4:15 to speak with a balance of truth and love.

Gift	Weakness	Neutral	Strength
Leadership			
Administration			
Discernment			
Wisdom			
Teaching			
Shepherding			

continued on next page . . .

Comments:

Core Competencies

The field of core competencies has its foundations in decades of industrial psychology, which developed in response to the advent of the modern corporation. As society moved from decentralized, small proprietorships to larger, centralized organizational structures (both in business and for nonprofit concerns such as educational institutions, hospitals, and government agencies), organizations demanded increasingly sophisticated management structures and effective managers.

The succeeding era yielded a treasure trove of insight into the inborn attributes that tend to distinguish the best leaders in any organization. The church, to its detriment, has ignored this source of wisdom. With the move to the more complex strategies required for small group infrastructure, it is essential to understand and use these proven tools.

Numerous leaders consistently exhibit some innate traits. Regardless of profit or nonprofit orientation, the demands of building and running the systems within organizations require some distinctive capabilities that tend to be longstanding qualities. They are not spiritual gifts—the divinely granted attributes people display by God's grace, which are not any person's doing—but they are personal attributes that take a long time to develop. Any organization, a church included, seeking key leadership to develop its effectiveness is best served by identifying a point person who has these necessary core competencies.

There are several helpful sources for tools and education on core competencies. Among those that are particularly focused on organizational leadership is Hay Group, which has grown into an international consultancy devoted to organizational effectiveness and leadership improvement. Hay Group offers a library of tools designed to educate, evaluate, and develop the managerial capabilities of the best leaders. (See *www.haygroup.com*.)

The following discussion will provide a brief initiation into core competencies, as applied to the church and its small group point leader. Distilled into a concise set, there are four core competencies that make the biggest difference in the best small group champion.

1. Conceptual Thinking

Think of the question *what* to begin understanding what a person with conceptual thinking tends to do. With this competency in play, someone can be extremely comfortable sitting in the midst of complexity knowing they can figure out what is confusing to most people. They can crystallize the real issues and distinguish them from the red herrings that take others off course.

You can readily see why this competency suits a small groups champion well. Much of the work is highly conceptual and demands careful thinking about the nuances of people and systems, present and future, along with general church context and ministry alignment. The point leader has to interpret emerging trends versus unworkable approaches, distinguish salient data from irrelevant information, and envision how the abstract can become relevant.

2. Intellectual Curiosity

A point leader increases effectiveness through the trait of intellectual curiosity, which centers on asking *why*. This attribute means that someone is inquisitive, always digging for more. They will not accept the first answer as the real, only, or even best answer. There is constant wonder over "next": the next solution, the next growth source, the next trend, the next learning, the next idea, the next experiment.

Intellectual curiosity can make a remarkable difference in how a point leader guides the ministry. It prevents the point leader from falling into predictable response patterns to challenging questions. The intellectually curious point leader will inspire experimentation, dig for correlations between tactics and outcomes, and foster others' curiosity.

3. Strategic Orientation

How is the question that drives strategy. It turns knowledge into action. Strategy helps translate the activities of disparate individuals into organizational outcomes of great value. In the church, largely built through the efforts of numerous volunteers, this trait aligns people to vision and to others' efforts.

Due to the decentralized nature of a groups ministry, creating a "together outcome" from independent leaders who are being empowered to shepherd their little flock requires a point leader with a strategic orientation competency. Figuring out how to move people from point A to point B, and then C, D, E ... to Z—and not just logistically but spiritually—will press the *how* question into every discussion and decision. When the strategic orientation capacity goes down, idle activity goes up. Before long those who are following will feel their efforts may soon become futile.

4. Others Focus

In business parlance this capability is sometimes labeled a "customer service orientation." In ministry, an others focus means asking, early and often, *who*. As in, "Who will this serve?" "Who has needs that can be met with this solution?" "Who is ready to respond to the new initiative?" An others focus creates structure to serve people, not the other way around. It means the leader won't lose the plot along the way and will remind everyone involved that everything everybody does has to touch lives in meaningful ways, or it is not worth doing.

This core competency matters far more in building a life-changing small group ministry than it does in the business world. Every bit of connection, caring, discipling, and compassion is intended for people. Everything (theology, strategy, etc.) is to be done in service of others, the group members, unconnected people, and lost friends, neighbors, and family. The question of *who* is easy to answer, but must be asked constantly.

———

As people read these descriptions, the names or faces of individuals they know often come to mind. Core competencies tend to be naturally occurring traits that develop only over long periods. There's no short-term or magic formula for growing them. That is not to say someone either has them or they don't. They can develop incrementally through extended training (see the Hay Group resources), but when a church is selecting its point leader, there will be a correlation between the strength of these core competencies and the fruit of their efforts.

PROCESS TIME

Core Competencies of the Point Leader

Now that you have a simple, beginning framework for the concept of competencies and how they apply to the point leader, you can use these basic concepts to build on the assessment completed on spiritual gifts. Follow the same process as with those and, using the following chart, consider the core competencies of your current or anticipated point leader. Based on your interaction and observation, where would you place them on the strength–weakness continuum?

Core Competencies	Weakness	Neutral	Strength
Conceptual thinking			
Intellectual curiosity			
Strategic orientation			
Others focus			

Comments:

Personal Factors: Experience and Spiritual Life

The first two segments of our discussion of point leaders have focused on spiritual gifts and core competencies. Spiritual gifts are out of the person's control; God decides who gets what. Core competencies aren't that fixed, but the individual only has so much control over those traits as well. Weakness in one or more of the important capabilities can improve with extended time and effort. In the meantime, others, who humbly team up with them to supply what is missing, will have to compensate for some of the shortfall.

The final segment, personal factors, is different, because each of the two categories we now describe will change over time, often much, and sometimes relatively quickly. A person's experience and their spiritual life are largely under their control.

Experience

This is not just ministry experience; it is experience at *building*—building a ministry, a business, a nonprofit, or another organization, building that requires strategic design, infrastructure and systems, processes and outcomes, and teams, whether paid or unpaid. That kind of experience at building an enterprise will be an indicator of how the point leader will do at building a life-changing small group ministry.

Although small group ministry does not correspond exactly with a marketplace or other nonministry context, it shares enough in common with any effort to arrange people, design functions, devise and revise plans, and monitor performance that the functions can translate. How to translate marketplace principles into church life will vary, depending on the experience of the point leader you select. Leaders must make a diligent effort to avoid the pitfalls of labeling these principles as purely "secular" or "sacred." Wisdom derived from multiple disciplines will help. Therefore, exercise caution before hiring a young guy graduating with a spiritual formation seminary degree, as opposed to a godly, mature, and wise expert at growing businesses and services.

Most of the time the experience will win. There is no substitute for having been there and done it, which makes sense when you consider the example at the beginning of this chapter. None of us would hire a children's pastor without a substantial track record of effectiveness at meeting the needs of children and their families. Likewise, a church would never hire a new music leader without knowing their experience in music, leading bands, and facilitating worship. The same principle applies to small groups.

Since the primary task is to build a churchwide system for connecting and growing people and their relationships, the point leader must have at least some analogous experience. Until the church has been immersed in building such ministry for a couple of decades, many of the new point leaders will migrate from related fields and use their business experience to benefit the church.

There are an increasing number of ministry veterans, both staff and volunteer, who have enough experience in building a life-changing small group ministry that your church may be able to find someone with transferable experience. However, even with such candidates, be extremely diligent to assess their tangible experience at building the kind of ministry your church is counting on. A candidate's experience doesn't have to be a perfect fit, but do not ignore how their story may contribute to the developing narrative in your setting.

Healthy Spiritual Life

The point leader's spiritual life is critical for two reasons. First, this person will be a model to the congregation of the life to which he or she is calling others. When it comes to small group structures, the modeling qualification is all the more urgent, since your church wants to reproduce in its future leaders what it sees in the life of its point leader. This leader represents a developmental, self-replicating leadership strategy.

This role is, perhaps more than any in the church, a 2 Timothy 2:2 role. "And the things you have heard me say in the presence of many witnesses entrust to reliable people who will also be qualified to teach others," said Paul in his parting mandate to his protégé, Timothy. These words move deeply into the consciousness of the point leader, and there are few leaders who will have such an overt opportunity to make them actionable. What they say about spiritual life done right, about spiritual leadership exercised well, and about spiritual reproduction sought perpetually, brings the health of the point leader's spiritual life to the fore.

The second reason the point leader's spiritual life is important is because they will need fuel to sustain their ministry. Every minister marches out onto a spiritual battlefield requiring appropriate divine preparations, but anyone who chooses to champion small groups is building the very church Jesus predicted would beat back the gates of hell. Every little community formed will be in a fight for people's souls against a deceitful enemy bent on destruction. He won't take any discipleship initiative lying down.

In addition, the point leader has what could well be the toughest job to sustain. The senior pastor has a pretty good idea when weekend services are over what kind of feedback he is getting in response to his primary job requirement. Worship leaders plan and execute their jobs on a weekly basis, and know within a range what will work well for the congregation's experience. Children and students aren't shy about telling their parents and leaders how they are doing at their jobs, and regularly.

Contrast that with the small group point leader's world. These leaders won't know whether they made the right call until two to five years have passed. Since most of the impact occurs in decentralized settings, it will be hard to know how things are really working. The point leader shares leadership with numerous volunteers who will have plenty of ideas about what could be done better, but few feedback mechanisms for timely responsiveness. Nobody knows for sure whether the point leader really is doing the right thing day in and day out since there are no weekly "performance cycles," as there are with senior pastors, worship leaders, and teachers.

All of these dynamics create a draining environment that will call the best out of the person who tackles this job. The ability to feed oneself spiritually and to maintain deep, consistent spiritual resources is an indispensable quality the church can't afford to ignore. The point leader must have plentiful fuel to sustain the spiritual battle with a strong sense of calling, passion, and joy.

PROCESS TIME

Experience and Spiritual Life of the Point Leader

It is time for the third cycle of evaluation of your current or anticipated point leader. Use the same approach as with the prior two, either individually or collectively. Based on your interaction and observation, where would you place the point leader on the strength–weakness continuum?

	Weakness	Neutral	Strength
Experience			
Healthy spiritual life			

Comments:

BRINGING IT ALL TOGETHER

In my experience, no church has successfully launched a cell system without averaging three turnovers of leadership. In other words, pastors typically flounder twice with each cell system start-up before they discern and train the right person.

—Carl George, *Prepare Your Church for the Future*

First, although there is a sequence to gifts, competencies, and personal factors due to the control someone has over their development, there is no sequence to how needed they are. Each of the traits discussed above has to be part of the initial and ongoing assessment of the point leader. You can shortcut one or more of the recommended qualifications, but it will be to your church's detriment.

Second, keep in mind that all of these characteristics will not be present in their entirety in any single individual. Strengths and weaknesses should be complemented by the person's relational equity within your congregation, their historical performance, the pace and nature of anticipated change in the small group ministry, and so forth. Intentional development or team configuration can compensate for small gaps in needed performance. However, the point leader's supervisor and peers serve nobody by being less than frank in the discussion about strengths.

PROCESS TIME

Summarizing Your Findings

Use the more comprehensive chart below to collect the varied feedback from a team engaged in the evaluation process, and then address the questions that follow.

Quality	Weakness	Neutral	Strength
Gifts			
Leadership			
Administration			
Discernment			
Wisdom			
Teaching			
Shepherding			
Core Competencies			
Conceptual thinking			
Intellectual curiosity			
Strategic orientation			
Others focus			
Experience			
Healthy Spiritual Life			

continued on next page . . .

Where does the point person need to develop or improve skills? What steps can we take?

In what areas do we need to shore up weaknesses through other staff members? What steps can we take?

POSITION THE POINT LEADER CLEARLY

Selecting the right point leader is paramount to ministry success. Even the finest leader, though, when poorly positioned in their role in the church, will encounter frustration and experience minimal effectiveness. Establishing the proper position for the point leader, then, is also vital to the success of a small group ministry.

Authority is essential in biblical leadership, and it must be properly distributed and clearly defined. A leader without biblical authority—humble, Christ-centered, others-focused authority—is incapable of providing the spiritual direction and making the difficult decisions required to advance the ministry cause.

Christ gave his apostles authority (Matt. 28:18–20), and they exercised that authority to guide the church, deal with challenges, declare the truth, and mete out necessary discipline. In a similar fashion, the point leaders will need the church to provide a clear description of the authority they have in this role, and how much they can delegate to coaches, group leaders, or others on their team.

We will consider two aspects to authority: influential and positional authority.

Influential Authority: Leading "Up" with Peers and Supervisors

Influential authority involves two critical factors: backing and "buy-in."

Backing

Make sure you have "backing" from senior leaders in the church structure. Elders, deacons, senior pastors, or other supervisors must stand behind the point leader and the group life vision. Without this, the point leader is left with uncertainty regarding the level of support behind the ministry.

Backing the ministry means supplying the essential resources for success in the following areas:

- *Budget.* Will funds be available for leader training events and for materials? Will the point leader be able to pursue ongoing personal development, attend conferences, or purchase materials to help in building and managing this ministry?
- *Position on the Leadership Team.* If this ministry is to have a churchwide emphasis, it is important for the group life pastor to be on the leadership team or have a regular presence there to provide progress reports and interact with key leaders. If the person is a volunteer with limited hours, at least provide interaction with senior leaders on a regular basis.
- *Platform Exposure.* Will the ministry and the point leader receive exposure at services and key church events? Does this just mean an occasional announcement, or will efforts be made to raise the value of group life churchwide? Will the point leader do some teaching or have some other leadership role from time to time in Sunday services so the congregation identifies him or her as a strategic leader in the church?
- *Strategic Information.* Will the point leader be apprised of appropriate verbal or written communications in the church between elders/deacons and senior staff? In other words, will they receive copies of board minutes or other documents that affect the context of their ministry? Be sure to provide the point leader with such information—like general budget issues, plans for facility expansion, key staff issues, or other churchwide information. This gives them credibility with volunteers as one who is "in the know" and allows them to make decisions that are in alignment—not at odds with—senior leadership and vision.

Buy-In

Make sure senior leaders also "buy in" to the philosophy and strategy of the small group initiative. If you are the point leader, do not assume that because you have *permission* to build the ministry that you have the buy-in from senior leaders and other staff or influential people. In order to gain rapport and get this buy-in, you will have to do some relational and strategic work to bring influence. The following are opportunities for influence:

1. *Look for problems to solve for others.* In order to prove you are interested in the success of the entire church and not just "your ministry" of small groups, assist others in understanding groups and how they might improve and grow their area of ministry, and help them solve any problems they encounter as they utilize groups. Is the student ministry having trouble finding leaders? Do serving teams need clarity about how to leverage groups to get more ministry accomplished?

2. *Look for how to serve others.* Perhaps the women's ministry is using groups but needs help designing a system to track who is in which group, who is leading, what they are studying, where they meet, and so on. You could help solve this problem with them. Every ministry needs assistance with training, communications, and event planning. By getting involved with each opportunity, you could serve them while influencing how their department pursues group life.

3. *Look for how you communicate with people.* Each person you need to influence has a distinct style of preferred communication. Some colleagues are emailers, while others rely on their cell phones. It may take a periodic breakfast with one person, a regular lunch with another, and in-office meetings with some people. Think of the occasional box of donuts you bring along for discussions not as bribery, but as good wisdom!

4. *Look for how to monitor progress.* The good news about group life is that it is measurable, so you can figure out how a leader or subministry is doing. The bad news is that if you use that information in the wrong manner, you will be perceived as the police department rather than the source of helpful aid. However, you can inspire passion for how a ministry is building community and then bridge to discussions of mutually agreed indicators of success. Once those are understood, both sides — the influencer and the influenced — can monitor impact.

Positional Authority: Leading "Down" without Damaging Relationships

Most point leaders in the church will find themselves in positions of influence. Some, because of church size or their own leadership capacity, will find themselves supervising other small group staff or adult ministry staff and volunteers. When you have a position "over" someone else in ministry, this relationship tends to function solely as a boss-employer relationship, which is not optimal.

In order to demonstrate that you are the leader of a highly functional team and dispel the perception that you are merely a boss barking commands to subordinates, here are some productive strategies.

1. *Set mutual goals.* By setting mutual goals with those whom you supervise you achieve a greater level of partnership. If you simply delegate or assign goals to others without their significant input, you set yourself up as a boss instead of a ministry partner.

2. *Identify and overcome mutual barriers.* Work together to identify sticking points for their ministry. What obstacles are in the way of building the men's ministry or blocking the efficiency of the food pantry? How can you help? And how can groups and teams be utilized for the solution?

3. *Increase the frequency of contact.* Do not limit interaction to an annual or biannual "performance review" with those you supervise. Frequent contact with people you lead builds the relationship, assures that they are pursuing the vision and mission alignment, allows them to share immediate challenges they are facing, enables you to assess their leadership progress or areas for development, allows you to wisely deploy scarce resources, and reinforces the overall team spirit.

PROCESS TIME

Point Leader Authority

Which type of authority does the point leader have? Which does the point leader use? What can be done to make sure they are positioned for success?

continued on next page . . .

FOCUSING THE POINT LEADER: CAUSE, VALUES, PEOPLE, STRATEGY

After positioning the point leader for success in the church, make certain there is clarity about the core practices of their ministry. Here are the four areas of focus for the point leader's work.

1. Declare the Cause

Clarifying and communicating the group life mission and vision is the point leader's first responsibility. As the leader, you must model the vision, embody it, and share it regularly with leaders and congregants. Make sure the vision is clear, compelling, and calls people to action. Whether at a lunch meeting, over a cup of coffee, in a class, or from the pulpit on a Sunday, you are the chief communicator of the group life ministry in the church. Others—especially the senior teachers—can help, but you are ultimately responsible.

Your tone, especially in public forums when you teach or make announcements, must express passion and commitment. You are not conveying information; you are communicating vision. When you are finished talking, listeners had better be clear, inspired, and convinced you really believe what you are saying.

2. Define the Values

Your team should be clear about the underlying values behind the group life initiative. Your values might include some of these examples:

- We believe community is essential for spiritual formation
- Life change happens in authentic relationships in groups
- Groups need leaders to guide the process and encourage the people
- Groups are places where truth meets life

These values cannot simply be shared with your core team; they must be reinforced from the pulpit so the congregation understands why groups are essential to personal spiritual growth and for building community throughout the church.

3. Determine the People

Team building is a regular practice of the point leader. Surrounding yourself with people who embrace the vision, share the workload, and help develop the strategy will bring strength and longevity to the ministry. That means investing in these people, loving them, hearing their ideas, caring about them as people (not just workers), and keeping them informed of strategic churchwide information and decisions.

Trust building is another unavoidable practice for anyone involved in relational work. People follow those whom they trust, but trust is fragile. It takes a long time to build and can be destroyed in a few minutes. On one occasion a group life pastor shared that he was having trouble getting buy-in to the ministry from the elders in his church. "I am getting tired of waiting for them to get on board! I am just going to go around them and begin building this thing on my own," he laughed, "and worry about getting permission later."

We advised him that if he chose this course of action, he might want to start working on his resume and getting his job references lined up, because he will probably need to seek new employment in a couple months. Working underground, avoiding difficult conversations, keeping information from others, using manipulation or power to get results, and blaming others for your own failures are easy ways to shatter the foundation of trust you were starting to build.

4. Deliver the Results

Implementing the strategy for building group life and making sure people move toward a common destination is your responsibility as the point leader. You cannot delegate this. You have to deliver on the promises, assumptions, outcomes, and life change, or the cause will be fruitless, the values unrealized, and people's efforts largely futile.

Clearly define success for the team. How will you know you are making progress? How many groups, leaders of groups, or people in groups will indicate you are moving forward in ways that signify progress? What indicators of spiritual progress will let you know that the quality of group life, not just the number of groups, is increasing?

Monitor progress by reviewing the ministry benchmarks—qualitative and quantitative. When a small group ministry begins to miss its goals, we call it "ministry entropy," and it can catch you off guard. Things appear to be going well and you begin to focus attention on nonessentials. You can be so busy finding new leaders you neglect to see if the connection strategy for adding new members is working.

Time flies and suddenly you discover there has been no teaching from the pulpit on groups, community, relationships, or leadership in the last eight months—not a message, an announcement, a story, nothing. You got lazy or sidetracked and entropy did its work. Vision drifts and people are talking about the "small group thing" in the church instead of "biblical community" or "group life."

Define success and guard against entropy.

PROCESS TIME

Point Leader Focus

Where is the point leader investing most of his/her time? Where is it most needed?

MANAGING THE POINT LEADER

As good as your church's point leader might be—the right one, rightly placed within the team, and doing all the right things—some unique management issues may emerge that will require them to enhance their effectiveness. The following sections of this handbook address two needs, first the need to lead the leader, and then the need for the leader to lead himself or herself.

Leading the Leader

Much of the foregoing discussion assumes the point leader will be able to devote full time to the small group ministry. However, in numerous congregations—for budgetary, strategic, or transitional reasons—the point leader builds the church's community life as a primary focus but must also complete other jobs. Without skilled management of the point leader's time, the urgency of other tasks will squeeze time allocated to groups. Overt and detailed discussion should help resolve this dilemma.

For starters, have the point leader track their time for two or three weeks so there can be a baseline on current activity. Bundle typical pursuits in several categories. The following table provides one example, summarizing average time allocation after several weeks' work:

Primary Job	General Activities	Hours Allocated
Point leadership	Initiate group ministry changes Recruit coaches and leaders Develop cross-department strategy	18
Systems administration	Design new training Place new group members Track data on group growth	15
Pastoral counseling	Maintain regular office hours Intervene with marital crises Provide post-service counsel	14
Family ministry oversight	Manage youth/children areas Solve weekly event issues Monitor camp experience plans	8
Short-term missions	Work with volunteer leaders Liaison with partner ministries Respond to member inquiries	5

By reviewing this table, both the point leader and their supervisor can learn a lot. First, totaling the hours worked shows that averaging sixty hours per week is an unsustainable pace regardless of the small groups initiative.

Second, a couple of the job assignments defy boundaries and limitations. Pastoral counseling needs persistently emerge, and following up after weekend children's and ministry event issues can't be delayed.

Third, it is going to take time to make the changes needed in order to prioritize the groups ministry, reallocate responsibilities, recruit volunteers for parts of the work, and revise subministry processes. The church has to plan for preferred work patterns.

Once you have established the baseline by monitoring the flow of a typical week's activities, you are ready for the management discussion about optimal time allocation. This will be a give-and-take process to balance desired outcomes with realistic demands, and planning for the transition from current reality to preferred future. The following table is an example of how the point leader's time and activities could be retooled, at least for starters (changes in italics):

Primary Job	General Activities	Hours Targeted
Point leadership	Initiate group ministry changes Recruit coaches and leaders Develop cross-department strategy	30
Systems administration	Design new training *Oversee volunteers by managing placement and data tracking*	5
Pastoral counseling	*Reduce regular office hours* Intervene with marital crises *Begin counseling referral system*	10
Family ministry oversight	Manage youth/children areas *Design monthly response system* *Delegate camp planning*	5
Short-term missions	*Shift responsibility for short term missions to semiretired board member*	0

As illustrated by this table, the goal is to create a point leader role that continues the needed division of duties and time, while reordering specific tasks, identifying new volunteer needs and opportunities, shifting responsibilities, and revising systems and processes. It also reduces work time from sixty hours to fifty—still a lot, but much more manageable. Everyone involved should hold loosely the actual implementation process, since the changes will take time, have to be modified along the way, and respond to periodic emergencies that will interrupt progress.

Leaders can manage the transition with ongoing weekly tracking. The point leader and their manager will then have the needed information to continue administering the transition that must happen for a divided job description to produce the desired outcome. Progress will ebb and flow and plans will require further fine-tuning, but a diligent effort will drive change.

PROCESS TIME

Leading the Leader

The table on page 71 is a reproducible chart for use in your setting; make multiple copies for initial assessment, weekly tracking, and collaborative discussions on needed changes.

Primary Job	General Activities	Hours Targeted

Self Leadership
Creating a Safe Community for Yourself

- *A place to be known.* Every leader needs significant, redemptive relationships to rely on and draw from. Leaders need community and should themselves be part of a group. Find the trusted friends who are able to treat you as a person, not as a ministry role or a spot on an organizational chart.
- *A place for stretching your faith.* Where will you stretch in prayer, in stepping into new territory in your walk with Christ? A group will help. It is here you will likely find two to three close spiritual friends with whom you can pursue a deeper life.
- *A place to pursue spiritual growth.* We need people who will "spur us on to love and good deeds," as the Bible encourages. Point leaders must pursue spiritual growth if they are to lead others with integrity. You don't have to be "more spiritual" than everyone you lead; but you must be intentional about having a personal growth plan you are seeking to follow. The plan, when discussed and prayed through with trusted friends, can be a tool for development.
- *A place to be affirmed.* We each need to be able to say, "I am broken, but I am loved." At times this is difficult to do, so we need others who will say it to us and for us. "Encourage one another," says 1 Thessalonians 5:11, "and build each other up." Do you have a regular place to build up others and have your own soul lifted up?

Managing Your Personal Schedule

Each of us has the same amount of time each month to accomplish life. The challenge is how to allocate our energy, resources, and attention to the right things at the right time in the right amount. Most ministry-minded pastors and church volunteers are in way over their heads with obligations to work, family, ministry, local community, school, volunteer organizations, sports, and whatever else gets thrown at us.

How do you monitor your energy level and ensure that you are creating space for personal rest, solitude with Christ, and life management? The chart in the process time section on page 73 is a tool that might help. It is a simple and quick way to get a pulse on your allocation of time and energy to those things that matter most and energize your soul.

PROCESS TIME

Leading Yourself

In the following table, there are twenty-one boxes, each representing a chunk of time, morning, afternoon, or evening, seven days a week.

1. If you have an obligation (not a personal choice to use free time) that exists in a box, place an X over the entire box. For example, you have to be at work Monday through Friday, 8:00–5:30 each day. Put a large X in each of the ten boxes representing Monday–Friday, morning and afternoon each day. Do this for any other time period.
2. Be sure to place an X over a box where you have any obligation at all, *regardless of length of time*. That's right, a forty-five-minute meeting with the neighborhood watch team, a fifteen-minute call to a small group leader, or the thirty-minute orthodontist quick checkup for daughter Susan at 7:30 Monday night means putting an X across the entire box.

The reason you cover an entire box for even a "small" obligation is that any obligation takes emotional and physical energy, often lasts longer than expected, takes time to drive or walk to, and interrupts the rest, recreation, or quiet time you would otherwise schedule.

Make one copy of this page for each week you are willing to evaluate, and then fill in the chart below for your most recent week(s) of activity.

	Mon	Tue	Wed	Thu	Fri	Sat	Sun
Morning							
Afternoon							
Evening							

How many boxes have you placed an X over?

20–21 = You are headed for burnout
18–19 = You live in a high-stress zone
15–17 = You are busy but likely productive
10–14 = You're probably on vacation
6–9   = You're retired!
1–5   = Get a life!

When you live in the near-burnout or high-stress zones for too long, relationships, work, health, and the soul all suffer loss. You end up with a destructive life pattern.

So how do you prevent crashing and burning, and avoid operating under constant self-imposed stress? Here are some suggestions key leaders through the ages have used to build a lifestyle that is challenging yet sustainable over the long haul.

Sustainability: Managing Life at Warp Speed

1. Monitor Your Gauges

Spiritual. How am I doing with connection to God and times of solitude for prayer, Scripture reading, and reflection?

Emotional. What is the condition of my soul and the quality of my relationships? Is there conflict, tension, unresolved pain, anger, or just a depressing kind of weariness? Or am I feeling very connected and do I have a clear conscience?

Physical. Am I eating healthy food, managing my weight, getting ample rest, exercising, and going to recommended checkups for my season of life to monitor my health and gain the information I need for ongoing health management?

2. Three Keys to Sustainability

1. *Set boundaries.* Boundaries allow you to say yes or no to any given request, demand, or opportunity. By understanding your limits and clearly structuring priorities, you are able to respectfully, but truthfully, say "No, thanks," to a situation. How many nights will you be out of the home for work or ministry commitments? When is the day really "done" for you?

2. *Create margin.* Margin is unscheduled space on your calendar for rest, family, reading, friendships, specific time alone with God, or whatever else you'd like to do—even nothing. Having margin allows you to carve out moments of time to spend *as you please.*

3. *Replenish your reserves.* What refills your emotional, physical, or spiritual tank? Whatever it is, and assuming it is nothing illegal or immoral, do it! Filling the body and soul with fresh energy and renewed vision will keep you and your ministry alive.

What is your strategy for setting clear boundaries, carving out necessary margin, and replenishing diminished personal resources? If you do not have a plan, busyness and obligation will rob your soul.

BEING THE RIGHT POINT LEADER THE RIGHT WAY

Being the point leader can be one of the toughest jobs in the church. Sizing up a leader's gifts, capabilities, experience, and spiritual life is essential. Positioning well, doing the right things, and managing both the work and life itself are simply parts of the job.

A point leader who is up for the challenge can make an incredible impact that will ripple into leaders and lives for all of eternity, in exponentially multiplying ways. Every cent paid, every plan formulated, and every effort to enhance the point leader's effectiveness will prove worthwhile for the church willing to invest in this critical role. It will set the stage for all that follows: structure built well, leaders deployed for impact, and groups gathered to flourish.

UNIFIED STRUCTURE

Implementing a Coaching Strategy

THE NEED FOR STRUCTURE, LIKE IT OR NOT

"Community and structure are incompatible!" Whether people say it or not, that's what some think. Idealists love the idea of groups forming throughout the church in ways that are relational and organic in nature, self-leading and self-sustaining.

But here's the truth: highly organic and flexible organisms are usually quite structured, though.

The question is not, Should we have a structure? Rather, the question must be, What kind of support structure should we have? What will empower your leaders and support them for optimal ministry and personal effectiveness?

Biblical Examples of Structure

In Exodus 18 Moses sought to adjudicate the affairs of Israel, handling complaints and legal disputes by himself. He was the chief provider of wisdom. Thankfully, his father-in-law, Jethro, was much wiser. He watched closely as Moses and his people were increasingly drained and frustrated while Moses heard each dispute.

"Case #23,467; Jacob the Benjamite vs. Seth from the tribe of Judah. The plaintiff accuses Seth of insufficient payment for the sale of twenty goats. State your case and call your witnesses!"

On it would go for days. Jethro finally offered a structure and a strategy. Here is the biblical account from Exodus 18:14–26.

> When his father-in-law saw all that Moses was doing for the people, he said, "What is this you are doing for the people? Why do you alone sit as judge, while all these people stand around you from morning till evening?"

> **KEY QUESTION**
>
> How do we support and care for our leaders?

Moses answered him, "Because the people come to me to seek God's will. Whenever they have a dispute, it is brought to me, and I decide between the parties and inform them of God's decrees and instructions."

Moses' father-in-law replied, "What you are doing is not good. You and these people who come to you will only wear yourselves out. The work is too heavy for you; you cannot handle it alone. Listen now to me and I will give you some advice, and may God be with you. You must be the people's representative before God and bring their disputes to him. Teach them his decrees and instructions, and show them the way they are to live and how they are to behave. But select capable men from all the people—men who fear God, trustworthy men who hate dishonest gain—and appoint them as officials over thousands, hundreds, fifties and tens. Have them serve as judges for the people at all times, but have them bring every difficult case to you; the simple cases they can decide themselves. That will make your load lighter, because they will share it with you. If you do this and God so commands, you will be able to stand the strain, and all these people will go home satisfied."

Moses listened to his father-in-law and did everything he said. He chose capable men from all Israel and made them leaders of the people, officials over thousands, hundreds, fifties and tens. They served as judges for the people at all times. The difficult cases they brought to Moses, but the simple ones they decided themselves.

Jethro basically says, "Create a system of groups and leaders. Share the ministry and the responsibility. Reserve your strength and energies for what you do best. If the case is too difficult and cannot be handled even at the highest level (of thousands) then you, Moses, can apply your unique wisdom and discernment to the situation. Everyone will be better off."

Brilliant! Groups of people sharing the ministry load, seeking to resolve conflicts with each other under the discernment of a capable leader. It made sense and was life giving. The result: a healthier leader and a more stable community.

The New Testament also offers a structure for the community—a system of elders and pastors and others who function as a leadership group, ensuring that the churches function with spiritual health and maturity. (See Acts 6 and 1 Timothy 3 for the use of groups and leaders to bring order and spiritual discernment to issues.)

> The structure serves the people—the people do not serve the structure!

Structural Metaphors Bring Structure to Life

The greenhouse metaphor beautifully integrates structure and organic growth. The piping, glass, and electrical wiring for heating and cooling a greenhouse constitute a structure that, while not very attractive, is essential. What goes on inside—organic, dynamic plant growth—is fostered by this structure. Few people remark, "Wow! Did you see that greenhouse? Incredible wiring and very effective glass panels for allowing light to enter!"

Inside the greenhouse, ingredients for growth are applied and the plants are protected from harm. The structure allows for light and temperature control, as well as protection from harsh elements like wind and snow. Don't forget the other essential element to growth: the gardener.

The gardener intervenes in order to facilitate optimal growth and to remove weeds or other threats to the emerging life within the greenhouse. Watering, fertilizing, and pruning are essential for sustainable growth and health. The gardener removes some plants and sprays others with herbicides to protect them from pests and diseases.

A group life ministry is like a greenhouse. Inside these life-giving groups, leaders and members enter the process of growth and development in an environment that makes such growth possible. The Holy Spirit, the Word of God, prayer, worship, and other spiritual activities keep the group moving forward.

The leaders of such groups need the support of a coaching structure. Coaches (or whatever name you choose for the role) will engage the leader much like a gardener does a plant. Coaches provide encouragement, resources, protection, prayer, and whatever leaders need for success. They also correct or remove a leader who is destructive or a threat to the group (a rare occurrence that usually requires church staff to intervene).

The coaching structure could also be compared to the skeletal system in the body. Providing structure and support to the body "behind the scenes" keeps the body in alignment and sustains the other, more organic systems (circulatory, nervous, digestive, muscular, etc.). The other systems purge waste, protect us from disease, bring essential nutrients to tissues, and regulate overall well-being. Yet, they would all collapse without the support of the skeletal structure.

Structure That Makes Sense

It is common sense to support leaders with some kind of structure. Coaches, functioning like biblical shepherds, ensure that leaders are cared for and empowered for ministry. You invest a great deal of time in the shepherd-leaders of groups; don't squander that investment by not supporting them with a viable structure.

How many coaches and leaders should a healthy structure have? What is the ratio of coaches to group leaders? What is sustainable, and how do we implement a model or approach that works? Well, first let's tackle some obstacles that might stand in the way.

PROCESS TIME

Obstacles to Building Coaching Structure

If you have tried to build such a structure before, list some of the problems you have faced. Or ask your team what they believe have been the barriers. If this is new for you, what do you think might be potential roadblocks to building and sustaining such a structure?

1.

2.

3.

4.

BARRIERS TO OVERCOME

In our experience, here are some of the common and most threatening barriers to building a structure for coaching and shepherding group leaders. Understanding them, and then evaluating which ones are holding your church back, will ignite progress.

1. Neglecting the Priesthood of All Believers

Without knowing it, many of us undercut the ministry of so-called lay people because we believe in the following adage: "If you want something done really well, let the professionals handle it."

In an attempt to protect volunteers from taking on too much, or from getting in over their heads, we primarily give them ministry responsibilities that are low risk and low skill. While a noble motive, your best volunteers end up under-challenged, distracted by lesser causes, or devoted to ministries other than yours. Coaching dramatically empowers lay leaders in ways that ultimately test how this doctrine fleshes out.

We do not have the time or energy to make the necessary investment to develop volunteers, so we just assume they cannot grow into it, and we do it ourselves or hire a staff member. The cycle of professional ministry reinforces itself all over again.

Sadly, we are only keeping emerging leaders from demonstrating their potential to shepherd others, and we rob them of the joy of the substantive ministry and personal transformation that occur only when we take the leadership risk. The first obstacle may be staring at you in the mirror. Ask the person looking at you about his or her theology.

2. Point Leaders and Church Staff Become Distracted

Coaching leaders is not imperative. It's important and strategic, but almost never urgent. So developing a coaching team can slip to the bottom of the "to do" list and another month elapses without making an investment in people that will pay off months from now.

The sources of distraction come from multiple directions. Senior pastors don't perceive the managerial shift needed. Parishioners want staff to meet care needs rather than focus on mentoring key leaders. Calendars call for seasonal activity, and existing programs continue on autopilot. The urgent wins.

Developing coaches will force job description analysis, program evaluation, priority shifts, and time management discipline like few things in ministry will. Unless you pursue the important, nothing will change. Will you?

3. An Emphasis on Events over Execution

In an effort to streamline our training and development work, we decide to increase the number of leaders we can put in the room and decrease the amount of personal investment in them. The logic goes somewhat like this:

"If I can develop five leaders, why not thirty-five? Instead of doing seven meetings with five leaders each, why not just have one meeting with all thirty-five? After all, it is the same content!"

This makes sense if you are preaching to a group or teaching the chemical and biological process of photosynthesis. You can give tennis lessons to twenty people; but a good tennis coach is focused only on a few. When you are developing leaders and working in a relationship-heavy environment, personal involvement and modeling the ministry are fundamental to the development process.

Events—an important aspect of leadership support—are no substitute for personal time, prayer, and investment in a leader's ministry, life, and family.

A coaching structure is a strategic development tool. Execution on the strategy—developing coaches who care for and shepherd group leaders—cannot be neglected in favor of events, as catalytic and inspirational as they may be.

4. Coaches Doing the Wrong Things

A leading obstacle to progress on coaching is the failure to define the precise functions and optimal contribution coaches deliver. Make sure the ministry role of the coach is clear and that they receive ample training and support for that role. Remain focused on helping them do their primary ministry.

Often church leaders get sidetracked, recruiting their coaches to help with the evangelism campaign, or do membership interviews, or attend unnecessary meetings. Like other volunteers, coaches have limited time each week to fulfill the ministry of shepherding leaders. Do not compromise their time with busywork, filling out reports, and setting up chairs for the next big event.

5. Misunderstanding the "Communication-Development" Continuum

Never confuse communication with development, or teaching with training. Information transfer is not the same as skill development or learning spiritual disciplines together. Church leaders must make a decision.

Will your strategy be heavily developmental, giving each coach three to five leaders to work with, or will it be heavily weighted toward communication and idea sharing?

Here's the continuum:

Development ———————————————— Communication

On the "Development" end of the continuum, coaches can only work with three to five leaders on average. Time spent with leaders is essential, especially with newer or inexperienced group leaders.

On the "Communication" end, dozens of leaders can be "coached" because the primary job of the coach (often a staff person or part-time paid role) is to connect and support a large number of leaders. Meeting one-on-one with all leaders is impossible, so coaches spend their time primarily with ministry crises or leadership challenges. They use email, social media, classes, events, and other gatherings to inspire and inform group leaders, but very little actual coaching takes place.

It is important, therefore, to decide how many leaders you want each coach to support. The greater the number the more informational the ministry will become, as opposed to a developmental approach.

THE ROLE OF THE COACH

Coaching need not be complicated. Yes, it requires effort, but it can have a few simple focal points. We outline a threefold approach in *Coaching Life-Changing Leaders* (by Bill Donahue and Greg Bowman). Call it "3-D Coaching" if you'd like.

Discover = a snapshot of what God is doing in your life and ministry. The focus here is on prayer and listening to God, and connecting with the leader about spiritual issues, personal life, family, key relationships, and group ministry. Questions include:

- How are you doing?
- How is your soul? (Weary, strong, connected with God and others, etc.)
- What can we pray about?
- How are things with your family and other key relationships?
- What is happening in the group or in your leadership role that I can be praying about?

Develop = a focus on specific challenges to address and opportunities for growth. Here we engage with issues or problems, personal and group growth, or new leadership skills to explore. Items for discussion include:

- Spiritual disciplines to explore
- Leadership issues and ideas
- Group problems
- Problems with specific group members
- Opportunities for adding new members or new study materials to use

Dream = getting our eyes on what God is doing in our lives and in his kingdom. God has a vision for the church, for building community and for advancing his kingdom mission. This part of coaching seeks to align the lives of leaders with the greater purposes of God. This is an opportunity to dream together, pray, and ask:

- What might God be doing in the lives of group members that we can encourage?
- How is God creating passion in our group for people and for ministry?
- What is God doing right now in our local church that we can pray about?
- What is God doing around the world?
- What might God do in our personal lives? What are we asking him to do?

What Leaders Need from a Coach

We have surveyed group leaders and their coaches to determine what needs focus and how the ministry can improve. We are very clear about the biblical mandates to call people to follow Christ, to connect them to his body, the church, and specifically to a community that fosters growth and service, and to raise up people for ministry as leaders.

It is not always clear how to do this. Some hear the word *coach* and envision a football or basketball coach shouting directives from the sidelines and evoking fear among the players. Coaches in a small group ministry, however, are more like tennis or golf coaches, bringing feedback, strategies for improvement, and connection with key resources for personal growth.

Coaches need support, training, and regular communication if they are to be effective at shepherding leaders. Below are five clarifications regarding how you develop coaches to do the right things.

1. Emphasize Nurturing over Mentoring

Mentoring language implies an expert bringing years of wisdom and insight to an emerging leader. If you are building a law firm or consulting business, or if you are a new elementary school teacher, you'd love to learn the ropes from someone who has been there long before you.

By contrast, to nurture someone means to encourage, support, and build them up to do the ministry at hand. You do not have to be an expert small group leader to coach others, but you need to be interested in the ministry of encouragement and prayer for a leader. You need to have been a group leader so you understand the context of small group ministry, but it is not necessary to have been the best group leader. (Again, think tennis and golf. Coaches in these sports are often less talented than the world champions they coach.)

2. Focus More on Shepherding Than Leadership

Everyone wants a pastor — either formally or informally. Our research shows that group leaders want a shepherd more than a "leader" if leadership is understood as highly directive and hierarchical. When a leader approaches a coach to talk about his son's challenges with drugs, he is looking for a pastoral connection, not medical advice, not personal expertise (your kids might have never been involved with drugs), and certainly not judgment or a patronizing tone.

No, he wants to be with someone who cares, who will pray and walk alongside him during the difficult journey ahead. Coaches have the great privilege of doing such ministry with small group leaders.

3. Emphasize Frequency of Connection with Leaders More Than Impact

The *presence* of coaches is more important than hearing a *presentation*. Rather than having long, high-energy meetings three times a year, encourage coaches to connect briefly and regularly with leaders. This can take place at weekend services, in a neighborhood, over a cup of coffee, or through email or a text message.

Frequency builds trust because you do not have an agenda when you see people frequently. If I only coach my leaders at events two to three times a year, I need lots of structure, some teaching, and a focused agenda. I need to emphasize mission more than relationship. Ongoing connection allows me to focus on the person and then to occasionally talk "business" with them.

4. This Is a Ministry of Encouragement More Than Management

Coaches are cheerleaders, encouragers, and a group leader's biggest fan! The goal is not to identify everything that is going wrong, put the spotlight on what to fix, or address why something is broken. Of course there are times for that. The coach's primary role is to bring life and hope to a leader who is likely discouraged or weary from doing ministry.

A manager focuses on quality control, efficiency, productivity, and organizational results. Though a church strives to achieve desired results and do it effectively (we are not minimizing such things), the ministry of coaching is more about encouragement than management. An encourager looks for the best in someone and brings that out. When someone is scared or overwhelmed, we remind them of their gifts, calling, and position in Christ, as well as our belief in them. Look at Paul coaching and encouraging Timothy:

> But you, man of God, flee from all this, and pursue righteousness, godliness, faith, love, endurance and gentleness. Fight the good fight of the faith. Take hold of the eternal life to which you were called when you made your good confession in the presence of many witnesses.
>
> —1 Timothy 6:11–12

> For this reason I remind you to fan into flame the gift of God, which is in you through the laying on of my hands. For the Spirit God gave us does not make us timid, but gives us power, love and self-discipline. So do not be ashamed of the testimony about our Lord or of me his prisoner. But join with me in suffering for the gospel, by the power of God.
>
> —2 Timothy 1:6–8

5. This Work Is More Spiritual Than Organizational

Coaches begin conversations with spiritual insights and topics, helping group leaders connect with God and follow his Spirit as they live and fulfill their ministry. Plans, strategies, numbers, reports, events, administrative issues, and other logistics are important but secondary to the spiritual development of people.

Train coaches to think "people first, institution second," and you will be fine. No one wants to sit across from a coach they have not seen in two weeks who begins the conversation asking, "Do you have your monthly report?" or "How many of your group members are coming to the retreat? Have they registered yet?" These are institutional priorities, not personal ones.

Optimizing the Coach-Leader Relationship

Here is a tip for helping coaches and leaders get the most out of their relationship, personally and in accomplishing ministry objectives. When defining and explaining their roles, make sure they are all in the same room listening!

We used to speak with leaders about why they have and need a coach, and then talk to coaches about how they shepherd leaders—but we never talked to them at the same time *about their relationship and ministry roles together*!

When you teach about the roles, coaches hear, "Now leaders, this is why you have a coach. Every leader needs encouragers, cheerleaders, and partners in ministry in order to be successful ..."

And group leaders hear, "Coaches are here to serve our group leaders, connect them with the best resources, introduce them to other leaders, pray for them and with them, and be a sounding board for leadership issues, problems and prayer requests."

Ask them to talk with one another about their roles, their expectations for their personal interaction, and how they will do ministry together. It makes a huge difference!

Coaches Reproducing Leaders ... and New Coaches

As you invest in a durable ministry structure, the goal is to not just choose coaches, but to grow, reproduce, and multiply leaders and additional coaches. Two key principles can help churches to achieve that:

1. Select the Right Coaches the First Time

Recruit coaches by relationship, not assignment. Work hard to select coaches who have some preexisting connection or affinity with leaders so the relational fit is strong. "Emotional equity" helps the coach to support the leader and the leader to *receive* care and input from their coach.

Ideally, a coach will be part of the effort to develop two or three apprentices who later become leaders. It would be natural to coach these leaders or have them work alongside current small group leaders, helping them raise up apprentice leaders who later lead small groups. As these apprentices become new leaders, there are more leaders to coach!

2. Find Coaches Who Prefer the Success of Others

Remember the metaphor of a tennis or golf coach. Look for people who have led good small groups in which people have flourished under their care, developed apprentices who proved to be successful leaders, demonstrated the solid relational intelligence servant leaders must possess, and do not have to be at the center of the action. Coaches inspire others to perform well, maintaining a behind the scenes role.

Any potential coach must find great joy watching other leaders succeed.

Key Coaching Practices and Coaches Toolbox

Refer to *Coaching Life-Changing Leaders* for a full description of these practices and the training to help coaches master them. You will find a rich store of resources and ideas to equip coaches in their ministry and to guide them as they serve small group leaders.

PROCESS TIME

Next Steps

What are the strengths and weaknesses of our current approach to coaching our small group leaders?

continued on next page . . .

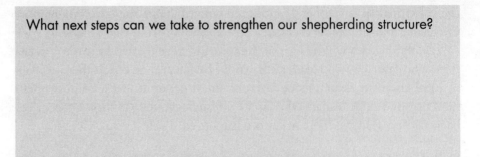

What next steps can we take to strengthen our shepherding structure?

Variations on Coaching

There are several approaches to coaching leaders, and implementing each one depends on a number of factors, including:

- How mature are the coaches both personally and in ministry experience?
- How seasoned and experienced are the leaders they are coaching?
- How developmental do you want to be?
- How often can you meet with leaders and coaches to equip them?

If there are many new leaders, or if you really want to invest in developing the leaders, then each coach will be able to handle fewer leaders.

If you are using the "communication" approach to coaching (remember the continuum earlier) then you can choose a method that coaches a greater number of leaders.

Look at the models below. Thanks to Dave Treat, our close friend and ministry partner for many years, each model is represented in a diagram below that clearly presents its strengths and weaknesses.

1. Developmental Model: 1:5 Ratio

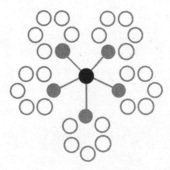

Strengths: The developmental model is a very robust approach that is effective throughout the life cycle of the ministry. The small group ministry can assign coaches to leaders, and there is a small span of care—each coach is responsible for only three to five leaders.

Weaknesses: Since you have a low ratio of coaches to leaders, you need more coaches and therefore must train more people for the role. Also, there is a tendency to choose coaches from among your best leaders, but they might be less effective as coaches because their specialty is group leadership.

2. Peer Coaching Model: One-to-One Mentoring

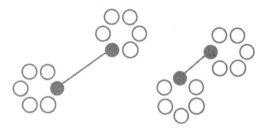

Strengths: When you do not have enough coaches in the ministry, leaders can coach one another. The peer coaching model can be a way to provide support and encouragement to leaders. They are not alone, and can pray for one another, solve common problems, and share ideas.

Weaknesses: Since the "peers" could be equally inexperienced, they might act as the "blind leading the blind" when there are more complex or difficult issues to address.

Note: This approach can develop into "Mentor Coaching" which simply means that one of the two leaders is more experienced and gives some of their time to mentoring a younger or newer leader for a season.

3. Mass Coaching Model: 1:25 Ratio (and Beyond)

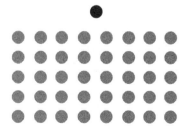

Strengths: The mass coaching model is effective for communicating vision and explaining strategy. With this approach you need fewer coaches.

In some churches these are paid roles (varying from a small stipend to a full-time position responsible for eighty to a hundred leaders).

Weaknesses: This approach allows minimal time for personal contact with leaders, unless someone were to do this role twenty to twenty-five hours a week and maintain twenty-five leaders or fewer. It creates a teaching and information-sharing environment and less of an opportunity to engage with leaders more frequently in personal settings.

4. Senior Coaching Model: Developmental Model Expanded

As coaches mature and can take on more ministry responsibility, you can have "coaches of coaches" or "senior coaches." (No, these are not coaches in Florida who work primarily with senior citizens.)

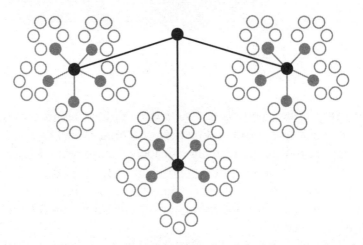

Strengths: The senior coaching model adds another layer of leadership to which experienced leaders can rise. If people are not going to be on staff, yet are capable of handling more leadership responsibility and more groups, this works. This approach limits dollars spent on hiring staff.

Weaknesses: This adds another layer to the structure and may increase the "distance" from senior leadership to group leaders and members.

5. Coachless or "Hands-Free" Coaching Model: No Specific Coach

Some leaders are very experienced and already serve as mentors to newer leaders. They are committed to the ministry, highly respected, and very good at what they do. Their need for coaching is minimal. They might not require an "official" coach to connect with them; but they still want connection, resources, and participation at retreats and large events. They need frequent communication, but don't need the kind of coaching most other leaders require.

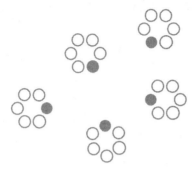

Strengths: The coachless coaching approach allows you to strategically deploy coaching resources to less experienced group leaders in the structure.

Weaknesses: The experienced leaders may develop a "lone ranger" mentality, working independently and drifting away from the core of the team. Also, this approach takes mature leaders out of the support system, and new leaders never get the chance to benefit from their wisdom.

A SUPPORT STRUCTURE THAT PAYS OFF

Every time your church invests in coaches and infrastructure, it does more than just care for leaders, give volunteers increased opportunity, or make your church more functional. The system ensures that group life will be sustained.

Coaches become the glue that holds "the temple" — to use one of Paul's favorite metaphors — together in ways that outlast mere sticks and bricks. They function as the ligaments and tendons that make "the body" stride with strength and speed. Coaches make the difference between church done as a professional work and a congregation becoming "a nation of priests and kings."

Implementing a coaching strategy will profit every leader and group attached to the support structure. Make the most of it and you will make all the more of our next topic: developing leaders.

Chapter 4

LEADERSHIP DEVELOPMENT

Developing Leaders Who Develop Leaders

KEY QUESTION

How will we reproduce leaders?

After working with hundreds of churches, we distilled the key issues they faced into seven categories that, if ignored or mishandled, cause ministry breakdown. We've recast them here as positive attributes that drive ministry fruitfulness. Clarity of vision, point leadership, and coaching, if pursued as described, will produce a sustainable community enterprise.

The fourth topic in the sequence, leadership development, will strengthen a congregation for a long-standing run of groups. Once a church unleashes an army of effective small group leaders, it has produced an engine of growth and sustenance that will be hard to stop. This is where we begin to build a church against which the gates of hell will not prevail.

CREATING A LEADERSHIP DEVELOPMENT CULTURE

The starting point for a small group leadership *system*, one that will generate leaders for the long haul, is a culture shift. The reason is simple but startling: a fully functioning church of small groups will put between one-fourth and one-third of the congregation into some stage of leadership development. On average, one in eight will actually lead small groups. Coaches will oversee the leaders, and they will in turn prepare a next generation of leaders in training. Other leaders will provide and supervise training or support functions. No matter how you analyze it, there will be a lot of people leading.

Imagine a discussion at your church's next board meeting asking them to provide a highly confidential list of leaders they feel are currently qualified to shepherd a group of adults. If you asked them to name names, the exercise would go something like this:

Alex: considered the best lay leader in the church
Bonnie: Alex's wife, who some actually would place ahead of Alex

Colin: a tremendous member with a lengthy list of roles
Danielle: well known as a shepherd, so would be a good small group leader
Earl: marketplace roles indicate good potential
Fiona: a Christian counselor who wishes the church would start care groups
Gaston: a board member who blushes when his name is mentioned
Hermine: she would be perfect to lead a small group for high school girls
Igor: has been leading neighborhood Bible studies, so could help train
Julia: a professor who facilitates graduate cohorts, a good model for groups and coaching

One of the board members suggests Karl, leading other meeting attendees to gasp because they have witnessed some relational immaturity in a few casual interactions. Similar reactions ensue with Lisa, Matthew, and Nicole. By the time discussions about Otto, Paula, Richard, and Shary are done the board is starting to realize how few leaders are ready to tackle a small group. Tomas, Virginie, and Walter don't measure up either.

When somebody names that first person over which a board member cringes, and after that point the board is tapping into decreasingly attractive candidates for the shepherding roles it envisions, they have exposed the problem most churches share: they have fewer prepared leaders than they think.

Every church in which we've done this exercise finds little more than 5 percent of the congregation ready to lead. Even the best churches will probably identify less than 10 percent as qualified to lead.

The gap between the leaders they have versus the leaders they need defines the shift a church must commit to when they embark on expanding the small group ministry. A church that moves into the small groups business is simultaneously moving into the leadership development business.

The church must become a place where leadership is normal and developing leaders is routine. Apart from this culture shift, the church never will realize its vision of community.

How does a church shift to a leadership development culture? The following activities offer some helpful pointers.

Teach and Model the Priesthood of All Believers

Shared ministry that is meaningful and challenging is the best leadership development tool at your disposal. You have to believe that people in the church are capable of leading.

"But you are a chosen people, a royal priesthood," says Peter to the church (1 Peter 2:9), echoing the variety of angles through which the Bible depicts orthodox Christianity. Sadly, the priesthood of all believers is often a belief but not a practice.

The indictment is not intended to be glib or condemning. It is factual. Most "priestly duty" in today's church, whether leading, teaching, administering sacraments, caring for the sick, or praying for the needy, is primarily the function of the professional pastorate.

Small group ministry changes that dramatically. Groups give legs to the priesthood of believers, more than any other ministry where people are asked to be a leader, teacher, pastor, caregiver, or intercessor.

Small group leaders are first on the scene when crisis strikes. They hear the doubts of the wavering and extract wayward sheep from the thickets.

Your church will have to teach the biblical priestly functions so that both the shepherds and the sheep understand the fundamental shift in how you are doing church. You will need to repeat an increasingly familiar statement to your small group leaders: "You are the pastors of our church." Your leadership culture will need to become a priesthood culture through everything the church teaches and models.

Champion the Leadership Value

Leadership is a corollary to community. The value placed on community must be accompanied by an equally strong value on leadership. Leaders matter. God raises up leaders when needs arise, uses leaders to do his bidding in our world, deploys leaders where action should start, and gets behind leaders who are faithful to their calling. A reproducing leader ignites a legacy of recurrent ministry that only heaven will fully reveal.

The tide of how most leadership roles are filled within most churches has to be reversed. The typical approach to volunteer ministry is seasonal, so that most recruits consider any commitment to a role as a tour of duty.

Minimal commitment timelines do not work with most small groups. Members get their hearts knitted together, lives become a tapestry of shared experience, and people belong to one another. Novice group participants eventually become protégés and then leaders in their own right. Small group ministry is rarely seasonal and leadership is never just a tour of duty.

Championing the leadership value requires shifting from seeing it as a tour of duty to seeing it as a lifestyle. A church will deploy small group leaders who integrate their ministry into life and their life into ministry. They come to learn the rhythms of days, weeks, months, and years so that they can sustain their efforts over the long haul.

"Don't Just Teach — Lead!"

The reference point for many small group leaders will be the Sunday school teacher. Sunday school has a century-long history of amazing ministry through which many adults received remarkable Christian education. Even those who didn't benefit from such classes often received similar training through catechism, confirmation, or comparable processes.

Yet a small group movement in your church is more than a class. Many leaders will see themselves more as discussion facilitator than shepherd, more Bible study guide than pastoral minister.

Small groups foster far more life-on-life action than most classes. Consequently, small group leaders are far more than teachers. They lead people's *lives*. They model community and leadership development. They demonstrate how leadership and leadership development are supposed to work.

Your church needs to communicate regularly that small group leaders cannot just teach; they have to *lead*. In developing a small group ministry, the church puts in place a network of key influencers who will exercise the kind of watchful care the Bible envisions and Jesus demonstrated through the three years he devoted to his disciples. When he commissioned ordinary people to make disciples, teaching others was a part of the mandate, and the command has always been to teach others *to obey all he commanded*, which requires life leadership to individuals who are being transformed into Jesus' image.

Explore and Explain the Leadership Role

Merely hearing the word *leader* will give plenty of emerging small group shepherds the shakes. When they hear it, they think of Rick Warren, Andy Stanley, Bill Hybels, Ed Young, or some other celebrity megachurch pastor. These high-profile leaders have been a sheer blessing from heaven to the church, but they are not the model for small group leaders.

Leader is also a common term in the Scripture's discussion of spiritual gifts. Someone pondering small group leadership might conclude they are not qualified if not in possession of the spiritual gift of leadership. Your church will need to clarify the difference between the leadership *gift* and leadership *roles*.

Most parents do not have the spiritual gift of leadership, but for decades they lead in the most intensive leadership development setting possible. Within their neighborhoods, companies, schools, clubs, and community organizations, many of your small group leaders fulfill leadership roles, though they vary widely in their giftedness.

As you teach and discuss leadership, watch your language to be sure people are hearing about roles, not gifts. Help everyone see the enormous privilege God gives to a broad range of people, most who feel ill equipped to guide others' lives. Explain how their unique gifts emerge within a small group leader's setting. Show them from the lives of Jesus' disciples how a mistake-prone, doubting, and fallible band of young leaders called and anointed by the Holy Spirit can change the world. It has been said often: God doesn't call the equipped; he equips the called.

Weave Leadership Lessons into All Gatherings, Events, and Meetings

Recruiting the initial corps of shepherds requires a strategy. The church could invite people to gather after a church service to hear more about the need for a large number of new leaders. It could host regular events designed to surface the more mature from among the congregation in order to yield an initial harvest of needed leaders. These strategies, however, will produce a decreasing number of fresh sign-ups as time passes. The "low hanging fruit" will have been picked.

A leadership development culture shifts the way your church envisions emerging and eventual leaders. The discussion about leadership in public settings will increase and weave into routine platform conversation. You have to make leadership, aspiring to it, moving toward it, and developing it as *normal*.

Your senior pastor and other teachers will fall into a new rhythm with weekly messages. Instead of making a leadership appeal before the sermon, they can use an aside within a message: "Let me give a word to those of you who lead small groups within our church," they might say, and then devote a minute or two applying the message to small groups and their leaders.

Incorporating the leadership appeal into regular messages makes a far more powerful statement than any announcement the pastor might make. It clarifies for everybody that small groups and leadership are *normal*. It highlights that movement toward community and shepherding roles is *normal*. Over time it will become *normal* to weave leadership comments and explanations into every part of the ongoing commentary about how the church should function. Transition from the big plea for leaders and weave leadership into every conversation.

Personally Model Leadership Development

Talk is cheap. Leadership development cannot just be taught, explained, and clarified. Those currently in leadership roles—the senior pastor, other staff, board members, or ministry leadership—must model leadership development. What each of these individuals *show* about strategically and consistently expanding the leadership pool will reinforce what they have to *say* on the subject far more than mere words.

Creating the culture of leadership recasts each key existing leader into a new, primary focus. Every one of them must prioritize extending a hand to a few other individuals with leadership potential. They have to build routines and processes to connect regularly with the emerging shepherds, either one-to-one or as a group. Envisioning the leader in training, guiding their spiritual, relational, or organizational skill improvements, and preparing them to be deployed to do the same for others changes their future, the futures of those they touch, and the future of your church.

In the beginning, personal modeling of leadership development may tend to focus on those who are most ready to lead soon. Rather than simply harvesting those ripe for leadership, churches must learn how to grow new leaders—planting the initial kernel of belief that someone has potential, tending early growth, weeding out inevitable leadership mistakes, and preparing them to seed still more growth among a next crop of leaders. Jesus turned a Simon into a Peter, after all, showing for all time that the least likely can become the most impactful.

Imagine if the top ten current leaders in your church would each take three underprepared protégés through a year's process of intentional preparation to lead groups. The initiative would not only produce thirty new leaders. It would change the culture within the congregation more than any talk. Personally modeling leadership development transforms the mindset of both current and future leaders.

PROCESS TIME

Modeling Leadership Development

One of the keys to creating a leadership development culture in your church is for you to model that value personally. Whose future are you investing in? Can you name them? Do they know you are doing this with them? (If they don't, it doesn't count.) If you process these questions within a team setting, who should your peers take under their wing for a season? Who are the emerging, unidentified leaders your church could graduate into shepherding roles over the next year?

Making this happen involves three simple steps:

1. List the names of three people you are planning to develop.
2. Share your list with peers who can confirm your choices.
3. Decide on one step you can take within the next thirty days to develop each person.

Name	Step
1.	
2.	
3.	

LEADERSHIP SELECTION THAT WORKS

The future of your group life ministry hinges on one thing: leadership. The ongoing identification and development of leaders allows members to thrive and the church to grow. Where do you find leaders? What are you looking for?

We discovered years ago that selection is crucial; in fact, 80 percent of leadership success comes from selecting the right people. You aren't looking for "super leaders" who are itching to get a group and start leading, or for people with merely a pulse and some extra time on their hands.

How to Find Leaders

What kind of person are you looking for? Far more normal, unprepared, and reluctant folks than you might suspect … but seen for what they can become or how they might be effective if well deployed. You will find many of them through two simple avenues.

1. People You Know

Take some time to think about people you and your core team know. Do they have leadership potential? Have you ever asked them to join a process of leadership development in your church? What about groups in which you participate or the teams you lead?

Look at the list and determine who is ripe for leadership, who needs development, and who is disqualified. For those who are ripe to lead, start asking now. Generally they will say no the first, second, and even third time, but each time you ask a seed is planted or fertilized. It will blossom, eventually.

With people who need development you will go through a similar process just to get them started. They will start in due course, especially if you foster a leadership development culture. What do you do with them once they agree to start developing further? We'll provide you a tool to assess readiness and next steps in the next section of this chapter.

Keep an eye on the disqualified. Their situation may be permanent but may not. God is the master of second chances, redemption, unlikely comebacks, and resurrections.

Never say no for anyone. There is a lot more potential than you might dream.

2. Experiences You Create

The conventional strategy for finding leaders is: (1) find a potential leader, (2) recruit them, (3) qualify them, and (4) train them to lead a group.

There is another way. Instead of starting with a leader, let's start with a group—a community—and create an experience that might identify emerging or potential leaders. Do you recall what happened in Acts 6, when the apostles faced a dilemma concerning the feeding of the Greek-speaking widows in the newly formed church? These widows were being neglected during the food distribution as a primarily Jewish church focused on the Hebrew-speaking women.

The apostles charged the congregation to perform a task. They were to meet and pray and use their discernment, and then identify godly leaders to handle the task. The community already existed. Certain members had proven themselves over time in that community, at least enough to be considered for a special role. The same is likely true in your setting. Here are some specific strategies.

Super Group

The "super group" is simply a large small group (or medium-sized group) of approximately fifteen to thirty people, though it could be larger. Here is how it works.

Leadership: A couple or small team of two to four people can lead this. The goal is choosing people who can implement a simple strategy, create a warm, inviting environment, and facilitate a process that connects people and identifies leaders.

Process: The main objective is to subgroup the members for a portion of the meeting to allow more interaction and to provide opportunities for emerging leaders to guide a small group of people for a short time.

Format:

- Begin with a social time, some fun, and some refreshments or light food.
- Gather everyone together and take ten minutes to describe the evening so there are no surprises, at least for the first few meetings. Use an icebreaker to get people talking and getting to know one another a bit.
- Organize attendees into groups of four to five, and ask one person to function as facilitator. The facilitator has two responsibilities—to be timekeeper and to maintain the conversation (give each person a chance to speak).
- Give each facilitator a question or two related to the topic of discussion. When the people break into their little groups, make sure each has enough space to work. Assign groups to different rooms in the house or to corners of a larger room.
- Allow about twenty minutes for discussion. This will go longer as the groups get to know each other.
- Return to the larger group and debrief.
- Spend the last ten to twenty minutes connecting with people.

Strategy: The hosts or leadership team *do not* participate in one of the subgroups. Instead they "float the rooms" observing how things are going, handling any logistics or questions that arise. Specifically, they are looking for potential leaders. It may be the facilitator or someone else in the group.

Outcome: Each week the leadership team identifies potential leaders and asks members during breaks and social time, "Who was a good facilitator? Would you like them to facilitate again?"

Eventually a core group of facilitators will emerge and you can begin to train them. Ask them to arrive early for an overview of the evening, for prayer, and to brainstorm creative ways to lead this group or solve problems.

As smaller groups form, you can keep this strategy going, asking the facilitators to become the leaders of their groups, spin off the smaller groups and add people to them, or birth another super group from this one, sending eight to twelve people off to form the core of a new super group.

Quick Start Strategy

This is the high-speed version of the super group but can actually handle a larger number of people, especially if it takes place at a classroom in the church building. The entire process can be done in one ninety-minute experience or over the course of three or four weeks.

Strategy: People are invited to a group connection (or whatever language you choose) knowing they will meet people and try to form a group.

Organize people around tables of four to six as they arrive.

After some introductory comments, direct participants to take an interview sheet from the center of the table, identify a person whom they do not know, and pair up with them to be a team. Person 1 will now use the interview form to interview person 2; then 2 will interview 1.

Each person has four minutes to interview the other, recording information and answers on the sheet. Questions are simple and safe. "How did you connect with the church? Do you have other family? What do you do for work? Where do you live?" Some creative people on your team can come up with a few more.

After eight minutes, the leader calls time and instructs each pair to find another pair in the room, and then introduce one another. For example, since I interviewed person 2 (named Bob), I will say, "Hello this is Bob. He lives in Barrington and works as a manager for a clothing company. He has a four-year-old son and has been married eight years to Beth. He came to our church six months ago when he was transferred to the area."

Each of the four people will introduce someone. Now everyone knows three new people and has some information about each one.

Then the entire process is repeated. After about thirty to forty minutes, each person has met about six or seven new people, gathered some information, and then has twenty to thirty minutes to sit with any or all of them and continue some relationship building.

The worst that happens is that new people have met other new people, and some new friendships are beginning to form. People can sit at church together, get a coffee, or have some dinner and really get to know each other. In the best case, a group forms and begins the process of identifying a potential leader, setting a time to meet, and getting into the qualification process.

The approach is certainly quick, and we don't assume that deep community forms in thirty minutes. It is simply a way to facilitate the connection process for people seeking group life. Some churches are more intentional, actually forming groups for everyone who attends, and launching them into a six-week group experience with DVD curriculum or a study guide.

———

So now you have a potential leader who is facilitating a discussion. Are they ready to lead? What training do they need? How do you know if they can do this? What is the best training for them in light of their previous group experience and their spiritual maturity? Are they a wise, capable, discerning believer with lots of leadership savvy and maturity? Or do you have an axe murderer facilitating the discussion?

Here's how to assess the readiness of potential leaders.

How to Assess Readiness: A Three-Step Process

Our team's discussions on leadership selection have led to some concepts that Dave Treat transformed into the following flow diagram, which will give you a decision-making grid for placing potential leaders on the appropriate developmental pathway.

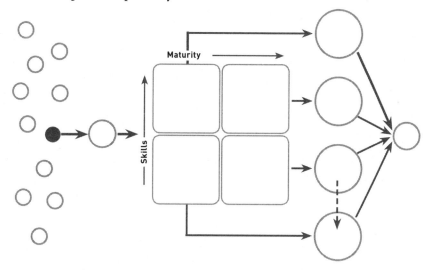

Step 1

Ask, "Are you in a small group?"

If the answer is yes, go to step 2.

If the answer is no, ask, "Have you ever been in a group, and, if so, please describe your experience, how long you were there, the focus of the group, and who was leading the group."

If they are not in a group in your church, find a group for them. Be careful about placing them in a leadership role too soon. They might be mature and even might have had a good group experience—but it was likely in another church culture with different values, expectations, and outcomes. You must judge the level of "risk" with which you are comfortable as you place anyone in a leadership role. There is always risk, and certainly we can be too cautious (remember who Jesus chose as apostles—not exactly the cream of the crop by most standards). Remember, you are placing a shepherd in a role with the sheep.

Step 2

As you continue in the conversation, determine where potential leaders line up with the decision-making grid.

(1) If a person is *mature/skilled*, they belong in the upper right corner. They have leadership experience in your church or other churches, or in business, for example, and they are also spiritually mature. All they need is some clarity about the role, some character references (if you do not know them personally, but others in the church know them), and some *vision* for the ministry. This is low-hanging fruit and ripe for the picking. Only about 10–20 percent of your potential leaders will have this background.

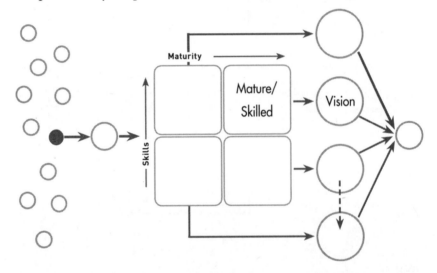

(2) As you meet another potential leader you discover he or she has leadership experience from the marketplace or a college team or in the education field, but is still a bit immature as a follower of Christ. They fit in the upper left corner of the grid—*growing/skilled*. What do they need before they lead?

They need a *discipleship* relationship in a group or in a one-on-one setting, accompanied by some classes, to ground them in the faith. This might require months or a year. It all depends on what your church requires as a baseline for leadership and how fast a person can demonstrate enough maturity to be entrusted with a leadership role.

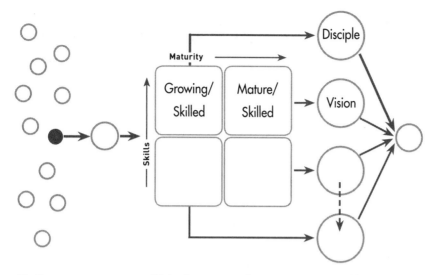

(3) Some prospects will lack essential maturity as well as leadership experience or skills. They would be placed in the lower left corner of the grid, in the *growing/unskilled* category. In an attempt to provide them with both—leadership development and basic discipleship—they can become an *apprentice* under a caring leader or with you.

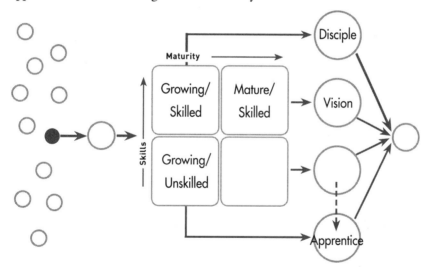

(4) Finally, there are people who are spiritually mature but you are not certain they have a baseline of leadership skills for guiding a group. They are *mature/unskilled* and need development. Chances are there are others just like them, so why not get them together and teach them how to be a group and how to lead a group? Carl George called these "turbo groups" because they

"turbocharge" the leadership development process. Instead of mentoring one leader at a time, you lead an entire small group filled with them.

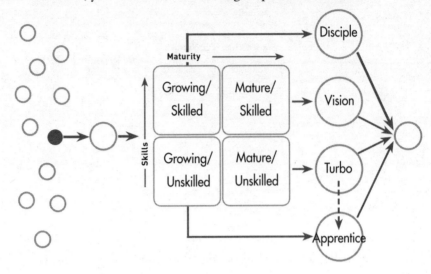

Step 3

Allow time for your observations.

It takes time to observe a potential leader and make sure they are growing spiritually and gaining the basic skills for leading a group. No one can tell how much time — it varies by person. Most are ready to lead in three to nine months if you assess them carefully and then channel them through the optimal process based on where they fit within the flow diagram.

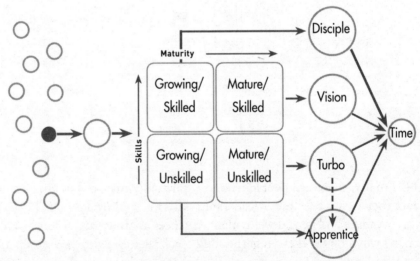

PROCESS TIME

Assessing the Leaders on Your List

Go back to the three names you listed in the Modeling Leadership Development exercise on page 99. In which of the four quadrants would you place each person? How does this impact the developmental step you wrote for them?

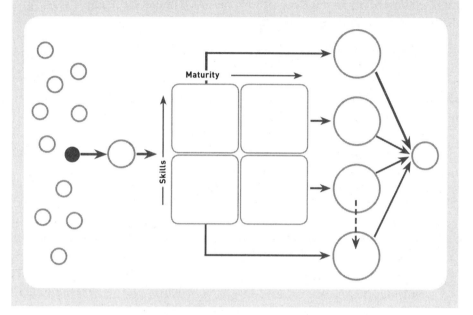

LEADERSHIP DEVELOPMENT STRATEGIES

Many churches that commit to building life-changing small groups will invest in leader training. The leadership training classes are well designed, but when their volunteers don't readily attend, the church is mystified about how to improve the outcomes. They tweak the seminars offered, even attempting to make them mandatory, and aggressively recruit attendees (always a questionable approach with volunteers whom churches won't fire over inevitable shortcomings).

Churches miss a couple of points in this process. First, any attempts to develop leaders without creating a leadership development culture or selecting and assessing leader readiness are set up to fail.

Context matters. Training classes offered *after* a new leadership culture is created make much more sense and are more likely to be attractive to volunteers who see how they fit strategically into the church's future.

The second issue every church must tackle when planning for leadership development is to radically expand its understanding of how elaborate "training" really is. Training is not simply a class. A life-changing small group ministry is built with a far more expansive framework in mind.

The Equipping Continuum

Every leader is a whole person. Training is not just a matter of prying open their brain and pouring in some information. Development requires a more elaborate understanding of how people change. Consider this simple diagram as a fuller picture of what growing leaders need:

Heart: inspire ⟷ Head: inform ⟷ Hands: instruct

Many churches are very good at adding to the information leaders have about how to lead small groups. That is not bad. After all, our mission is nothing less than imparting the very "mind of Christ." However, improving only the mind of a shepherd is not enough. What is the fuller range of what volunteers need? It pushes in two directions, on one side from head to heart, and on the other from head to hands.

- *Heart: inspire.* All of us know smart people who aren't very good at what they do. The problem is not their minds. They know enough. They are just not very passionate about what they do. Heart is about enthusiasm, a sense of calling and purpose. Knowing what to do is important. An underinformed leader who is filled with passion, feels as though they are on a God-given mission, and understands why their efforts matter both now and for eternity will have profound impact as their knowledge increases. Zeal alone will not cut it. Giving leaders more information in the hopes they will love doing their job won't either. Small group leaders require regular inspiration to stay engaged for the long haul.
- *Head: inform.* Well-schooled volunteers will be confident when deployed to shepherd their groups. Knowledge about how to lead well is not enough by itself. However, common mistakes are often a by-product of ignorance. It is up to you to inform leaders about how to do all they are being asked. "Inform" can never imply a simplistic download of a minimum amount of data, or a check-the-box sequence of receiving it. Ministering to the mind means helping every leader "get it," building awareness of the ins and outs of groups and people, increasing perception of the variety of issues they will face. It is a never-ending quest to get smarter, wiser, and better.
- *Hands: instruct.* No airplane pilot gets their license based on classroom information. Instructing emerging flyers requires more, in fact

a lot more, hands-on instruction than classroom schooling. They need both a classroom and an airplane. The much heavier emphasis will be in-flight training, though, which is why pilots use simulators to complement all they know to prepare for time in the seat. Leading small groups is a whole lot more like flying an airplane than passing a spelling test. What you have in your head is good, but what you do with your hands is life and death. This crude metaphor presses churches trying to develop good leaders to expand training well beyond some classes. A variety of instructional approaches will be required.

The Equipping Methods

Developing the heart, head, and hands of every leader involves three broader categories implemented on an ongoing, consistent basis. Each has strengths and weaknesses at inspiring, informing, and instructing, depending on the method, the volunteer's needs and learning styles, and the person delivering the development. Some of all, and all of some, will contribute over time to needed growth.

Coaching

Within the small group ministry lexicon, although coaching is a position within the ministry structure—as we have discussed for an entire chapter of this handbook—how coaching is implemented is more critical than having the job on an organizational chart, filled with the right kind of coach. Since we've already covered how to identify and deploy effective coaches, we will outline here the methods through which coaches engage small group leaders.

- *Connecting One-on-One.* By meeting with leaders they oversee on a regular basis—monthly is usually a good target—coaches can accomplish much with a leader. The agenda for such a meeting should vary, from a primary focus on care and prayer one month, to problem solving the next, and then to more of a mentoring or discipleship conversation another time. This should be a collegial, highly relational time, not a business meeting. Encouragement, cheering for leaders, and intercession are more the point, not supervision or accountability. If coach and leader are not becoming friends over time, something is amiss.
- *Gathering Peer-to-Peer.* Think "small group of leaders" with this method. A quarterly opportunity for leaders to be with peers will

serve many of them well, while not overdoing the schedule demand on the group. It is a prime occasion to envision, share ideas, practice skills, and accelerate their development. The same social and fun texture that groups enjoy should balance some serious times of mutual intercession or ministry information. Be sure to schedule far enough in advance to capture every leader within a coach's span too.

- *Visiting Meeting-to-Meeting.* Moving "on site" with a leader can help both coach and shepherd. By coming to a meeting, every group member is reminded about the commitment of the church to their care and to each leader's effectiveness. If there is passing awkwardness created by interrupting meeting rhythms once or twice per year, it is more than offset by the encouragement the coach can impart to the little community. By affirming the leader, experiencing the environment, evaluating apprentice potential, and sensing group life, a coach can improve both sides of the shepherding equation, for member and leader.

A transitional note: Carl George wisely remarked, "The higher the level of supervision, the less initial training is required; the lower the level of supervision, the greater the need for up-front training." Coaching can be critical as an equipping method, one that can fill gaps in formal training. The closer the coach, the quicker problems are intercepted and solved, the better development is tailored to leader need, and the deeper support flows from the shepherd of shepherds.

Coaching is not the only method of developing leaders though; equipping is *a variable method*. Each category—coaching, training, and supporting—works independently and collectively to grow volunteers' skills. How your church emphasizes all and each of them is a push-and-pull process, by ministry area and by leader.

Training

Unfortunately, *training* often automatically triggers thoughts of blackboards and desks, rote information acquisition, and a fixed starting and finishing point to the learning. When that is true, "training class" becomes redundant, a one-dimensional approach to imparting knowledge that fills more notebooks than lives.

Classroom learning is not inappropriate, but it is inadequate, especially for life-changing small group leaders.

Adequate training requires several delivery mechanisms to equip leaders.

All are legitimate and offer varied benefits, but with the benefits come limits, as depicted in the following table.

	Plus: Improves accurate assessment ↓	
Minus: Social immaturity caps potential payoff ↓	Self-study	Mentoring
	Classroom	On the Job
	Plus: Increases experiential learning →	
	Minus: Relational affinity limits optimal benefits →	

Self-directed learning, such as reading a book, viewing a video, or studying something like *Leading Life-Changing Small Groups*, plays an important role in leaders' growth, and provides the greatest potential to target specific developmental needs. However, the leader has no way to compare their comprehension or progress to other leaders as they can in a classroom setting, including accurate testing. Although a class improves potential assessment, personal dynamics affect learning. If an individual (including the teacher!) is socially underdeveloped—such as talking too much, lacking self-awareness, being withdrawn, or misguiding discussions—it affects not only their experience, but also the benefit that could accrue to others in the class. A bad encounter not only detracts from the lesson; it can take other students off course, even persuade them they want no further role.

Social immaturity can limit how leaders develop on the job ("OTJ training," as it is often termed)—shepherding their group—more than mentoring, too. A coach can identify and adapt readily to a leader's emotional deficits, whereas personality quirks or interpersonal issues (whether a by-product of a person's spiritual immaturity, emotional wounds, character flaws, or behavioral concerns) exponentially affect every person the leader is to shepherd. Accurate developmental assessment, though, is most precise when a leader can be evaluated in the real world of group life.

The small group setting provides the best curriculum for real learning in ways a classroom can't. Just as pilots have to use simulators and real planes to learn how to fly, small group leaders never really grow up in a classroom. The learning potential is limited when self-directed versus when aided by a mentor. Their experience can become their protégé's, who is spared mistakes the mentor has made already.

However, there are limits on mentoring and on-the-job education due to the relational nature of those settings. The affinity between mentor and student, and between group leader and member, will directly influence the shepherd's progress. Relational dynamics provide the incubator in which growth can either flourish or be stunted. Any compromise to affinity, whether in a mentoring or group relationship, will dilute the experiential learning quality and results.

Does that mean you forego the experiential learning opportunities? Of course not. Everyone involved in equipping leaders must facilitate the small group leader's growth journey well aware of the pluses and minuses at work in each method. The more a self-directed lesson or classroom learning can become experiential, through case study, observation, interaction, or role-play, rather than through basic reading, lectures, or rote information, the better it will be. The further a church can progress in helping to disciple even its leaders to get past character issues and spiritual or emotional immaturity, the better the learning will be in collaborative settings such as classrooms and groups.

When you "train," don't get stuck with putting together some classes. Include self-directed learning, mentoring relationships, and on-the-job assessment, in blended and varied form. Recognize the weaknesses and risks of each method, and compensate for them with both leaders and systems. Valuable training will equip leaders for a lifetime of increased effectiveness.

Further details on basic matters such as training topics and how they can be covered in the context of private, mentoring, class, and on-the-job settings are covered below, after further discussion of the full spectrum of equipping leaders.

Supporting

There are two additional activities a life-changing small group ministry must engage in on a consistent basis, both of which will complement your church's coaching and training efforts. Ongoing communication with leaders and periodic all-leader gatherings will contribute to a well-equipped shepherding corps.

Communication

Leaders need clear, consistent, and timely communication. Information about church developments, activities, and leadership concerns must be communicated with regularity. Group leaders and coaches are co-owners of ministry with you, and they require current information to keep members informed and to handle relevant questions.

The communication the church needs to receive *from* leaders is no less important. Small group leaders may encounter problems for which they need assistance (perhaps from both their coach and church staff), and these can provide unique insight into tactical issues the church or a department faces. Such issues may concern worhip services, children's ministry, how guests are treated, or a myriad of other non-small group topics. At a minimum, they need to be able to voice their support needs.

Do not get bogged down with the details of how communication happens best and miss these points. Sure, specific tools such as database tracking, group reporting, newsletters, bulletin inserts, and downloadable messages are important. Some churches find value in point leader blogs, Twitter, Facebook, and other, similar techniques. The moment communication becomes an end in itself rather than a quest to actually ensure an effective two-way exchange, you are not supporting your leaders. Communication done well—landing at the heart, head, and hands level when possible—will make coaching and training more effective.

Events

Most of us have worked in a professional setting, a growing organization, or a larger enterprise requiring shared vision and direction, so we understand how events serve everyone. Events can be catalytic, whether through continuing professional education gatherings, company rallies, departmental events, or planning retreats.

Events can generate passion, fuel recommitment, align ministries, unify effort, launch new initiatives, create common language, deepen values, trigger growth, and make shared memories. In a vision-driven ministry like small groups, leaders need the support you provide through such events, not mere coaching and training.

All-church leader gatherings can take the form of an annual or semiannual small group leaders retreat, a quarterly leadership community (before, after, or during normal church services), or a ministry year-end celebration. As an increasing number of churches adopt a group-based church strategy, there are more and more varied and creative approaches to such gatherings. Stay in touch with church-to-church networks, blogs, small group websites, and transferable marketplace ideas.

Ministry-specific connections include times when coaches gather with other coaches; when a department celebrates a ministry season launch or finish; when new leaders graduate; when groups launch new groups; when baptisms flow from a subministry's unique efforts; or when a team gathering leads to area-specific training sessions. All of these are examples of how a subministry can more precisely meet leader needs in ways a church's events cannot. Alignment—communication, coordination, and collaboration (as highlighted in chapter 1)—is critical for such gatherings' scheduling and participation.

Outside conferences provide training opportunities and can be places to build passion, values, vision, and ownership. A growing number of teaching churches, Christian publishers, parachurch providers, and key influencers are organizing, sponsoring, or collaborating to provide what few individual churches can create on their own. Some require travel, but many are now available via satellite delivery or on a more geographically dispersed basis. Perhaps your church can team up with other like-minded congregations in your town or region to develop what would serve many leaders well.

Supporting leaders requires methodical and persistent effort. When churches implement communication and events well, it balances the weight coaches and trainers must otherwise carry. Their ability to inspire, listen, envision, and inform is limited, in part, by the venues through which they play their role, and because of the uniqueness of small group ministry. Any church that moves into deepened community life must move into the communication and event management business.

PROCESS TIME

How Are We Equipping Our Leaders?

Now that you have the three methods for equipping leaders — coaching, training, and supporting — it is time to assess your current reality. Either individually or collectively, analyze what you have done in each area over the most recent ministry era, describe your church's activity as specifically as you can, and then specify how effectively each fit the continuum of inspiring, informing, and instructing your leaders. The following table is a tool you also can use to evaluate a specific department's equipping track record.

		What we offered this ministry season	Rate the continuum		
			Heart	Head	Hands
Coaching	One-on-Ones				
	Huddles				
	Group Visits				
Training	Self-Study				
	Mentoring				
	Classroom				
	OTJ				
Support	Events				
	Communication				

As you review the past ministry year, where are the developmental gaps in coaching, training, and support?

continued on next page . . .

Looking back, what steps could you have taken to improve what you did?

As you look forward to the coming three to twelve months, use the same framework to plan the next ministry season, utilizing the entire heart-head-hands continuum:

		What we will offer next ministry season	Rate the continuum		
			Heart	Head	Hands
Coaching	One-on-Ones				
	Huddles				
	Group Visits				
Training	Self-Study				
	Mentoring				
	Classroom				
	OTJ				
Support	Events				
	Communication				

Training Your Trainers

Though coaches are responsibile for equipping group leaders, a "training team" is also a valuable addition. Most churches do not make an effort to develop a cadre of volunteer training personnel, which is fine in the early days of transitioning the community. The point leader, senior pastor, and other key voices may be in optimal positions to signal the values shift and imbue the vision to founding small group leaders. Such a team can bring fresh ideas and creativity to the training experience.

As a small group ministry expands, the need for a training team becomes evident. Usually churches have a set of gifted individuals suited to this specialty, those who fit the Ephesians 4 description of "as each part does its work." Their unique part—to refine and expand the church's training capacity—is rooted in their history, gifts, interests, training, and professional backgrounds. Potential trainers could be found among veteran Sunday school teachers, college professors and school teachers, corporate trainers, consultants, life coaches, spiritual directors, and church staff, to name a few.

One essential move for churches that decentralize biblical learning into group settings is to redeploy those with spiritual gifts of teaching who have been displaced due to a reduced volume of centralized teaching venues. This high-impact team can help you retool the training you just assessed and planned.

As this team is formed, the church must train members in order to make successful use of their varied backgrounds, education, and experience *within the church and small groups setting*. Each one of them has to understand how all they've learned fits the church and the additional ground rules that will guide them in a ministry context. They also need to become experts at the skill set distinctive to small group leaders.

The Ground Rules for Church-Based Training

- *Nothing matters like immediate needs.* Any good trainer stays in touch with current small group leaders to find out where they feel underprepared. Not only will meeting that need equip them for the long haul; it will set them up to win with a small group that notes the increased maturity. Immediate application increases stickiness of the lesson.
- *A biblical foundation supports spiritual leadership.* Small group shepherds forget that Jesus is with them as they lead and joins their group whenever two or three gather in his name. The more often they can see

from the pages of the Bible or Jesus' own ministry examples of how to do what they've been called to, the more courageous and obedient to it they will be. Scripture speaks often into relationships, conflict, care, discipleship, and character.

- *Experience helps more than information.* The tendency toward talking heads, handouts, and PowerPoint presentations has to be reversed, especially to equip small group leaders. Everything they have to do can be reenacted, demonstrated, simulated, evaluated, and retried, whether after a group meeting or in self-study, mentoring, or classroom settings.

- *Stories inspire and motivate.* The case-study method frequents many professional courses, from medicine and counseling to business and law. Prior experience teaches principles students need to master for the similar situations they will live through. In ministry these are the stories that embody vision, reflect values, affirm noble work, and create hunger for similar results.

- *A tool or "pass-on-able" is required.* The "pass-on-able" is an old Navigators ministry concept. The basic idea: relate only what your hearers can reuse with someone they touch. When you train small group leaders, they are *always* in a position to touch a few others right away. Therefore, put a tool in their hand they can use at their next meeting; give them a great icebreaker, provide them an exercise, or furnish them creative study ideas.

- *Limit the download.* Do not try to teach more than two skills in any session. A well-tailored self-directed or mentor-facilitated lesson that actually embeds a single skill into a leader's heart, head, and hands beats covering several topics that hit or miss. Lower volume, more often, through varied avenues will work best.

- *The best training happens in stages.* There is no such thing as finishing the job. Shepherds can only carry a limited amount of unused learning in their backpack, especially what is received alone or in a class. It is best to anticipate what they will need over the next few months and then assume they will have to be resupplied later.

- *Leader maturity matters.* That means having to deal with the fluctuating audience you will train. Some will be untested rookies, many at intermediate stages, and an increasing number becoming seasoned. Then there is remedial training and corrective instruction. The training you provide will need to account for the complexity posed by what each already has learned, forgotten, or misapplied. Assess every audience well.

There is a treasure trove of transferable training capacity within your congregation, trainers who can share the equipping load if you will let them. Find them. Envision them well. Adapt them to the church. Deploy them often. Well-trained trainers can transform a leader corps.

Skill Sets for Life-Changing Leaders

As churches identify trainers and adapt them to equipping leaders, they need to teach them many skills. Group leaders will have to be lifelong learners if they are to leave the legacy God has in mind for them. There are diverse proficiencies to acquire, specifically tailored to the kind of group life you envision.

A variety of books and manuals can supply the lessons, some of which are listed in the Leadership Resources section below and in the *Leading Life-Changing Small Groups* handbook, which is a companion to this manual. You and your trainers will identify new categories, leader needs, and ministry initiatives, each requiring the creative formulation of how to impart that learning to your leaders.

Trainers can teach each skill in numerous ways, as displayed in the table below. The key understanding to draw from this is that redundancy is never redundant. Leaders need multiple avenues through which to absorb the learning opportunity, sometimes because one approach better suits their learning style, schedule, or readiness. It is likely they will assimilate the particular skill over time, so redelivery of a lesson from time to time can deepen their maturity.

This grid also permits planning, so you can monitor progress in developing a comprehensive training strategy. Don't be overwhelmed by the volume of subject matter, since this will not be built overnight. In fact, if you were not convinced of the need to train some trainers, this exercise will persuade you.

PROCESS TIME

How Will We Give Leaders the Skills They Need?

Start by sizing up your current offering of classes or other intentional skill development. If you evaluate your situation in a team, simply have each person check the box in which there are active initiatives. Once you compare your findings, you can discuss the rationale for your conclusions. Then use the table on page 120, adding your own skill sets, to plan for lesson delivery through multiple means.

Skill/Lesson	Setting			
	Self	Class	Mentor	On the Job
Basics of the role				
Inviting new members				
Preparing for meetings				
Choosing curriculum				
Icebreakers				
Leading discussions				
Guiding prayer times				
Fostering group safety				
Developing mutual care				
Casting vision				
Forming covenants				
Debriefing a meeting				
Temperament types				
Leading communion				
Group stages				
Marking moments				
Intentional shepherding				
Listening skills				
Deepening relationships				
Learning styles				
Forming good questions				
Conflict resolution				
Welcoming outsiders				
Socially stunted members				
Truth telling				
Group worship				
Using technology				
Identifying spiritual gifts				
Birthing a group				

Skill/Lesson	Setting			
	Self	**Class**	**Mentor**	**On the Job**
Developing apprentices				
Bible study skills				
Spiritual formation				
Leading change				
Launching compassion				
Pastoral care in crisis				
Group evangelism				
Church membership				
Subministry skills				
A lifestyle of leadership				
Tracking your legacy				

Ongoing Development

As leaders mature, it starts to dawn on them that even if they acquire all the skills in the world, there are still some challenges they cannot prepare for fully. We talked at length about this realization in our book *Walking the Small Group Tightrope*, in which we confront an often unspoken secret among leaders. Training can't solve all problems, and not all problems can be solved.

This "aha" was a by-product of some organizational study we had done on the subject of "polarity management," a concept conceived by consultant and author Barry Johnson. He gives permission to leaders to conclude that there are unsolvable dilemmas, in business and beyond. The reason? Often the issues that surface in various arenas are the by-product of mutually exclusive objectives.

Business owners have to charge their lowest price while making the most profit. Parents have to embrace and nurture their children while preparing them to exit their nest. Churches have to win over the unconvinced as they develop the already persuaded. In all these settings and many more, doing one and not the other isn't an option. *Both* must be done, which creates ongoing tension, an irresolvable challenge.

Small group life is filled with these tensions. While you can train leaders to solve problems, if you aren't honest with them that some problems never will be overcome, they will suspect you do not live in their world.

There are six specific challenges each small group leader faces, produced by six tensions — six sets of simultaneous "must-dos" that leaders can't avoid, not for long anyway. Stated positively, if they get used to managing the tensions, they will find not only the vibrancy of group life they want, but the pathway to a leadership adventure of a lifetime. What scares or frustrates them will come to be comfortable. They will be able to walk the small group tightrope between each of these tensions.

The Six Challenges	The Six Tensions	
The Learning Challenge	Truth	Life
The Development Challenge	Care	Discipleship
The Relational Challenge	Friendship	Accountability
The Reconciliation Challenge	Kindness	Confrontation
The Impact Challenge	Task	People
The Connection Challenge	Openness	Intimacy

You can access the *Tightrope* book for training content and for a small group curriculum leaders can use to introduce these concepts to a maturing community. But as you walk with your leaders on the journey of leadership development, introducing them to this sort of "graduate school" education on small group dynamics will provide a source of ongoing development. Lifelong leaders will be lifelong learners.

Leadership Resources

Over time, each small group leader will want to develop their personal library of resources to which they can turn as they prepare for meetings, shepherd members, and tend to their own development. The materials below are organized topically so you can point them in the right direction when they wonder about added resources for their group or ministry. You should be familiar with each of them and their content, too, as a ready response source when questions come your way.

Community

Jean Vanier, *Community and Growth* (Paulist Press)
Gilbert Bilezikian, *Community 101* (Zondervan)

Stanley Grenz, *Created for Community* (Eerdmans)

Dietrich Bonhoeffer, *Life Together* (Harper Collins)

Henri Nouwen, *Making All Things New* (Harper)

Stanley Grenz, *Social God and Relational Self* (Eerdmans)

Larry Crabb, *The Safest Place on Earth* (Word Books)

Stanley Grenz, *Theology for Community of God* (Eerdmans)

Small Group Ministry

Gareth Icenogle, *Biblical Foundations for Small Group Ministry* (IVP)

Jeff Arnold, *The Big Book on Small Groups* (IVP)

Neal McBride, *How to Build a Small Group Ministry* (NavPress)

Henry Cloud and John Townsend, *Making Small Groups Work* (Zondervan)

Small Group Models

Ted Haggard, *Dog Training, Fly Fishing, and Sharing Christ in the 21st Century* (Thomas Nelson)

Joel Comiskey, *Leadership Explosion* (Touch Publications)

Knute Larson, *The ABF Book* (Chapel Press)

Robert and Julia Banks, *The Church Comes Home* (Hendricksen)

Robert Lewis, *The Church of Irresistible Influence* (Zondervan)

Carl George, *The Coming Church Revolution* (Revell)

Garry Poole, *Seeker Small Groups* (Zondervan)

Ralph Neighbor, *Where Do We Go from Here* (Touch Publications)

Small Group Leadership

Bill Donahue and Greg Bowman, *Coaching Life-Changing Small Group Leaders* (Zondervan)

Neal McBride, *How to Lead Small Groups* (NavPress)

Bill Donahue, *Leading Life-Changing Small Groups* (Zondervan)

Carl George, *Nine Keys to Effective Small Group Leadership* (Kingdom)

Bill Donahue and Russ Robinson, *Walking the Small Group Tightrope* (Zondervan)

Leadership

Bill Hybels, *Courageous Leadership* (Zondervan)

John Maxwell, *Developing the Leaders Around You* (Thomas Nelson)

Patrick Lencioni, *The Five Dysfunctions of a Team* (Jossey-Bass)

Jim Collins, *Good to Great* (HarperBusiness)

Warren G. Bennis and Burt Nanus, *Leaders* (Harper)

John P. Kotter, *Leading Change*, (Harvard Business School Press)
Robert Clinton, *The Making of a Leader* (NavPress)
J. Oswald Sanders, *Spiritual Leadership* (Moody)

THE LEGACY OF A LEADER

As remarkable as it is to see one group function well for one season, that pales in comparison to the wonder of the ministry fruit one life can yield. In the introduction, we shared briefly about our stories and the big gulp it causes when we ponder a collective sixty-five years doing group life.

Although some of that is due to how fast time passes, when we ponder what one small group leader can do—guys and gals doing the ordinary routines of shepherding a group—it is stunning. We now have led dozens of groups, apprenticed scores of leaders, and birthed so many groups we've lost track. Those groups and leaders have in turn reproduced still more, while we continue, day in and day out, our shepherding rhythms. Given normal life expectancies, we may be only half done with what God might do through us.

This tale is part of every leader's emerging story. The unimaginable impact from every single life, especially if selected well, prepared thoroughly, cared for consistently, envisioned regularly, and resourced often is amazing. There are few more powerful engines of future spiritual life and eternal impact you can build. Its legacy will be without end.

Chapter 5

CONNECTION STRATEGY

A Place Where Nobody Stands Alone

A clear and well-executed connection strategy results in a life-changing small group ministry. The next three chapters articulate the essentials of effective connection of people to groups.

Think of them as legs on a three-legged stool. The first of the three concerns assimilation — shaping the pathways for connection. It is imperative to create clear pathways that guide people toward meaningful community. The two other legs of the stool — group variety and group openness — matter too. But the starting point for connection is diagnosing where people might fall between unidentified cracks.

DIAGNOSING THE CONNECTION PROBLEM

Bill and Mary, a new couple that just moved to your community, drive into the parking lot of your church for the first time. They are inclined to become a part of your church because it has a lot in common with their prior church, at least from what they can see on your website and have heard by asking folks in their neighborhood.

They want to find a church home relatively soon, since their prior congregation and its ministries have been of great help with their children, now aged fifteen, thirteen, nine, and six. Being new to town, they want to find friends for themselves and the kids, so identifying ways for everyone to belong is a big priority.

In the Process Time on page 126, describe in detail the steps that they will need to take, the interactions that will need to occur, in order for Bill, Mary, and the family to find their way from the parking lot into a small group.

KEY QUESTION

What are the pathways leading to group life?

PROCESS TIME

Mapping Your Current Process

Regardless of how refined your process is, for many churches Bill and Mary are assumed to move through steps that flow something like this:

Parking Lot
→ Main Auditorium
 → Newcomer Gathering
  → Class
   → Connection Event
    → Group

The steps and sequence may vary to some degree but most small group ministries will count on people moving through five to seven steps to find their way to a group. That is where the problem begins, not only for Bill, Mary, and their children, but also for the church they are trying to navigate into. You may think the sequence looks like the step-by-step, predictable sequence depicted above. Here is how it needs to be viewed to be evaluated accurately:

___ %	Parking Lot	___ %
___ %	Main Auditorium	___ %
___ %	Newcomer Gathering	___ %
___ %	Class	___ %
___ %	Connection Event	___ %
___ %	Group	___ %

The column on the left could be labeled "Percentage of Connectable Audience." That would be the fraction of those people at one stage who make it to the next staging ground for eventual connection. We assume those who decide to visit your church actually make it to the parking lot, and then can successfully make it into the sanctuary. So far, so good. But what if 80 percent of the "connectable audience" decides to move to the next step? That would be quite extraordinary, really, but let's assume a distinctively remarkable audience response. It would look like this:

100 %	Parking Lot	___ %
100 %	Main Auditorium	___ %
80 %	Newcomer Gathering	___ %
80 %	Class	___ %
80 %	Connection Event	___ %
80 %	Group	___ %

This looks good. That is, until you find out the label on the right column, "Net Realized Group Connections." Out of all those potential small group members that started in the parking lot or auditorium, here is the outcome:

100 %	Parking Lot	100 %
100 %	Main Auditorium	100 %
80 %	Newcomer Gathering	80 %
80 %	Class	64 %
80 %	Connection Event	51 %
80 %	Group	41 %

For most churches, there are more steps and fewer clean movements through them than we'd like to admit. We'd love to have over 40 percent of new guests making it to groups. If you wonder why you don't, this admittedly simplified illustration may begin to explain what is amiss.

The point is basic but significant: every handoff represents a potential drop, a crack into which someone falls. We're sure you have heard it as often as us. "I have tried again and again, and just can't find a group." Our steps often work better in theory than in reality.

If you study your connection strategy from Bill's or Mary's perspective, which really is the only one that matters, what are the barriers they find? How can you remove them? Where are people not making it from point A to point B? What gaps need filling? These questions and many others will begin to reform your assimilation process.

MONITORING THE PROCESS: IT'S NOT THE BUCKETS, IT'S THE FLOWS

Churches are good at buckets. A bucket is the place to catch people, such as a class or an event. When a special gathering goes well, it means there was a good turnout, people had a good time, and the staff or volunteers felt good about the outcome. However, good buckets simply don't indicate much about how a church will do at helping people connect with each other in life-changing community.

"Flows"—not buckets—are the primary concern of the group life ministry. Filling, watching, and evaluating buckets only matters to the extent a bucket helps move people into community. Assimilation, connection, belonging, whatever you want to name it, depends on the flow of people into groups where they find a place to belong.

More than a decade ago at Willow Creek, some members whom we consider assimilation experts volunteered some advice and counsel as we sought to connect people. One question remained central to their analysis—"And then what?" It helped us understand the actual flow of people in and out of groups and the flaws in our strategy at that time.

A note: We understand that a church the size of Willow is rare. This manual is not simply a description of our learning and experience at Willow, and we hope it offers some significant insights regardless of the size of your congregation. With the exception of some very small churches, many churches face common challenges in guiding people toward a meaningful experience in group life. The flow chart on the following pages might look complex—but actually it aims to be complete, not complex. Here is the result of the advice we received. It is not a recommended process but an example to learn from.

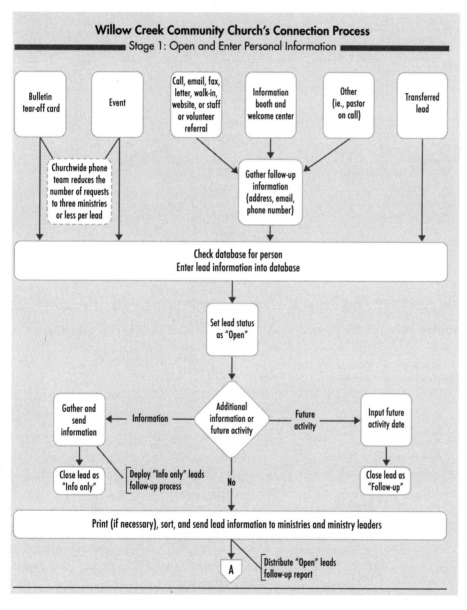

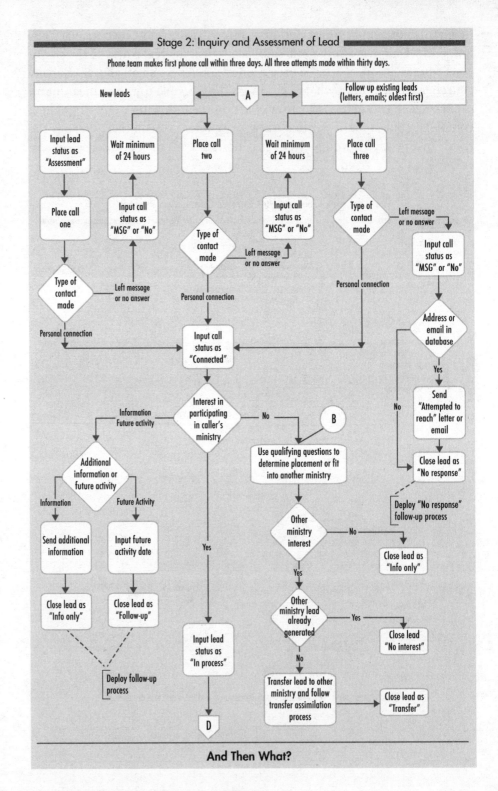

Stage 2: Inquiry and Assessment of Lead

Phone team makes first phone call within three days. All three attempts made within thirty days.

New leads — A — Follow up existing leads (letters, emails; oldest first)

Input lead status as "Assessment" → Place call one → Type of contact made → Personal connection → Input call status as "Connected"

Wait minimum of 24 hours → Input call status as "MSG" or "No" ← Left message or no answer

Place call two → Type of contact made → Left message or no answer; Personal connection → Input call status as "Connected"

Wait minimum of 24 hours → Input call status as "MSG" or "No" ← Left message or no answer

Place call three → Type of contact made → Personal connection; Left message or no answer → Input call status as "MSG" or "No" → Address or email in database → Yes → Send "Attempted to reach" letter or email → Close lead as "No response"

No → Deploy "No response" follow-up process

Interest in participating in caller's ministry → Information / Future activity → Additional information or future activity → Information → Send additional information → Close lead as "Info only"; Future Activity → Input future activity date → Close lead as "Follow-up" → Deploy follow-up process

→ No → B → Use qualifying questions to determine placement or fit into another ministry → Other ministry interest → No → Close lead as "Info only"; Yes → Other ministry lead already generated → Yes → Close lead "No interest"; No → Transfer lead to other ministry and follow transfer assimilation process → Close lead as "Transfer"

→ Yes → Input lead status as "In process" → D

And Then What?

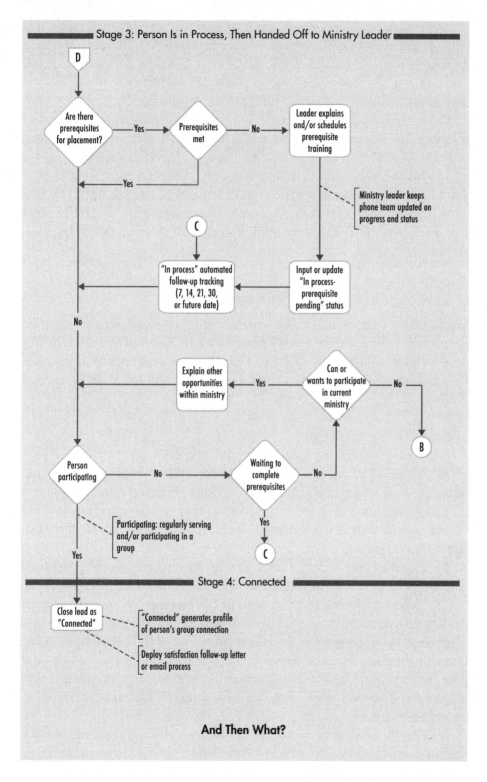

And Then What?

"And then what?" is a simple question that surfaces current reality. It is likely to produce a similarly complex diagram that will be very revealing. As you figuratively walk through the process from the perspective of Bill or Mary you will find there may be plenty of good ideas at work, but you have never connected the dots, conceptually or relationally.

Doing this in your setting could be a somewhat tedious process. Understanding flow is new to many churches, but they should nevertheless honestly assess how their process works right now. If you can see how people move into and through your church instead of just where they gather, it will begin the process of right conversation and process design. You will better discern the "migratory patterns" of your people and be able to reassimilate people into groups by helping them flow through the connection process.

CREATE A CLEAR CONNECTION PATHWAY

Moving from your current process to a revised, ever-improving strategy for connecting people to community involves a handful of principles that will produce measurable gains. Once you put them to work, improving people flow becomes possible. Make these your hallmarks for a well-designed process.

1. Make the Process Clear

It sounds obvious, but making the process clear starts with defining what "assimilation" means. When building a life-changing small group ministry, connection can only mean one thing: a person or couple joining a small group. Anything other or less than that is a stopping point along the way to the ultimate destination. Be clear with everyone, all the time, about the end game.

Making the process clear means getting down to very specific details. If you telephone people, how often, and when? Define it. Decide to call three times. Call once during the day, once in the evening, no more than once per day, or whatever; there is no right or wrong, just clarity.

Process has a tendency to degenerate into a set of tasks that, when done, result in checking some boxes. Clear steps must retain meaning and purpose. Keep reminding everyone involved in the assimilation process that it is about someone's mom, dad, brother, sister, daughter, son, neighbor, coworker, or friend.

Making the process clear includes defining and refining the role of every medium-sized gathering, such as a class, event, special occasion, retreat, and ministry initiative. These "buckets" are never negative unless they are done without clear intention. The positive contribution they make is enormous if everyone involved understands how to turn them into "pumping stations" that increase flow. You have to be—that's right—clear.

Be sure to define the *who*. Who is supposed to do what? Who owns each step of the change and takes responsibility for the outcome? Sometimes a process fails merely because someone assumes others are dealing with it. In a relational ministry, having an effective process means people clearly know their role in helping others take a next step.

Ask about what is essential and nonessential; what's working and what's not producing results. Every time you can remove a step, an activity, or a data point that is unnecessary, you streamline the process and improve flow. Analyzing the process will help you refine it, even if it is working reasonably well already.

You will find out how important it is to get information and track data. Names, phone numbers, email addresses, and accurate spellings become the treasure you can mine for rich results. Keeping the essential records, and nothing superfluous to what will aid assimilation, will improve the process. Keep track of it in the most useful manner for those who need it most.

Is the pathway clear to Bill and Mary? Is it clear to you? Clarity won't matter if it is not clear to them. Making it clear to them will make it clear to you!

2. Make the Process Simple

Start by reducing the number of steps in your process in every way you can. Our favorite example comes from North Point Community Church near Atlanta, Georgia. Although over thirty thousand attendees create complexity, their connection strategy remains a simple four-step process, moving people from auditorium to midsize gathering to small group. The North Point team has honed their process over time by providing a sophisticated support structure. For their Bill or Mary, though, the process is incredibly simple.

For example, North Point uses "GroupLink," a ninety-minute event where attendees connect with people in the same stage of life and area of town to form a community group. Community groups are small groups of six married couples or eight individuals of the same gender that meet weekly in a group member's home for fellowship, Bible study, and prayer. They are for adults of all ages, stages of life, and spiritual maturity.

During the first part of the evening, participants receive a warm welcome from the event host and a quick overview of what to expect. The evening consists of four parts: a thirty-minute mingle, group formation, a vision cast segment, and then the group launch.

- *Thirty-Minute Mingle.* The thirty-minute mingle is an opportunity to meet others who live in the same area of town. People spend time in conversation getting to know one another. Potential groups begin to take shape and friendships begin to form.
- *Group Formation.* During the group formation, people get better acquainted with the new people they've met and begin to form a group.
- *Vision Cast.* During the vision cast segment, everyone learns what to expect from a community group experience. They watch a video that takes a humorous look at what a community group is and what it isn't.
- *Group Launch.* To wrap up the evening, each group will sit back, relax, and get to know each other a little bit better. Members have some fun with some "icebreaker questions" and plan their first social event.

All this takes place in one gathering, allowing people to form initial connections and launch a group. It is a simple process for launching new groups.

The key is to increase process speed whenever possible. Churches gather information (or "leads," as salespeople say) from people with the intention to follow up immediately, but sometimes someone gets sidetracked and forgets the phone call. Garry Poole offers the best approach: after weekend services generate such data, he organizes a Sunday night pizza party for the volunteers who started making phone calls that afternoon and evening. The rule of thumb: "leads" go cold in twenty-four to forty-eight hours. Speed? Simple.

Creating a sponsor of the process can simplify your strategy. Churches have tabbed people with gifts of hospitality or helps for the role of *connector*, a person who is responsible to take the hand of an unconnected person or family until someone—namely a small group leader—takes their other hand. An insider to the process simplifies what an outsider cannot see when looking in.

You do not always have to invent something new, though. As you map your process, you might find an existing, but underused, activity that could produce connection results. Since people are already used to the ministry or event, simplicity might suggest improving what you are doing already instead of creating something new.

Communicate your process with simple, clear language. Always opt for simplicity and clarity over creativity and "buzz." Be consistent with verbal announcements and printed materials. Help everyone involved in the communication process reckon with how critical simplicity is to an unconnected audience.

A neglected aspect of the connection pathway has to do with movement of people who were formerly or are currently connected. People will move within your church, for lots of reasons. Singles get married. Support and recovery group members move on. Children graduate. We know these things but do not always account for "transfer assimilation" or reassimilation. It is simpler to anticipate such movement rather than move them into groups after someone has become disconnected for long.

Simplicity is the ally of clarity. Every step you take to make things simple for those who are trying to understand your system will aid the process of connection.

3. Make the Process Accessible

Access is key to initiating people flow. It starts with identifying entry points, places that most naturally lead to a step toward group life. Some opportunities will be seasonal, such as the start of the school year or the attendance bump you get after Easter and Christmas. Pay attention to ministry entry points that generate flow. For your church it might be women's Bible studies or classes, the preschool you operate, or periodic music events.

Provide trial experiences, so people can take a taste of community. People are more likely to commit to initial four- to six-week experiences or a semester-long group than an indeterminate suggestion they "join a group." Be sure the ending points on each experiment are clear and simple, so the initial effort pays off in the longer term connection each person really needs.

Discern productive pockets of flow, such as a high school ministry that pulls in a mom or a dad, a financial education program best done in groups that may continue after the seminar, serving opportunities that attract more volunteers, or sports ministries to which members bring friends who could transition to a team and then group experience. The place of primary access for one person can be a secondary entry point for those your church won't touch other than through the initial relationship.

Beware of "tired ideas," which are the approaches that once worked well, but do not yield the connections they formerly did. Almost every ministry tactic will tend to become an end in itself, sometimes because the proprietor of the event or methodology comes to own it at a deep but biased level. Passive, "you come to us" approaches over which you are disappointed are a sure sign of diminishing returns.

Did you notice that each method in the flow above—a connection event, class, or newcomer gathering—is centralized? Making group life accessible, however, may work better on a decentralized basis. A subministry special event (such as a children's gathering designed to make it easy for parents to connect, which we mentioned as an example above) may work better for some newcomers.

Involve group leaders in the process of creating accessibility. Some churches use a directory of open groups and provide a quick connection for people to an existing group. A church website is a great tool for making this happen.

You will probably get 50 percent of your adults in groups by having a clear group life strategy and a point leader. If your groups actively connect their own members, and your leaders and apprentices are working to connect people, you might get 60 percent in groups.

The sizeable remaining audience, whether new or old, will be connected by ongoing, persistent assimilation, transfer assimilation, and reassimilation efforts. A clear, simple, and accessible connection process, pursued with vision and passion for everyone engaged in community life, can open a door for every person.

PROCESS TIME

Maximize Your Opportunities

What steps will you take to increase the clarity, simplicity, and accessibility of your connection process in order to leverage your weekend services to the maximum potential?

	Next Steps
Clarity	

Simplicity	
Accessibility	

INCREASE THE PEOPLE FLOW

Once you have improved your connection pathway by implementing the three suggestions above, your church has a handful of readily available means to open some spigots for increased flow toward community. As you will see, much of the upgraded volume you create involves more fine-tuning than invention. Most of it is about releasing buckets of contained individuals who simply need to be pointed in the right direction.

1. Utilize Weekend Services

The largest gathering of people at any given time of the week is likely your weekend services. Rather than view these gatherings as separate from your connection process, consider using such gatherings to encourage next steps toward group participation.

Churches have used a variety of strategies, and here are a few to stimulate your creativity.

- *Directed Seating.* Sometimes you can direct or invite people to sit by geography or some other natural affinity whereby they can meet people. For example, by sitting in geographic regions the same people will see friends regularly, see people from their groups, and clearly recognize visitors.
- *Table Seating.* Churches whose worship venue does not have fixed seating can rearrange seats around tables. When the service is over, people can spend ten to fifteen minutes in a brief small group experience discussing the message and getting to know each other.
- *Greet and Connect.* Some use the greeting time during the service. Instead of simply shaking a few hands and sitting down, provide three or four minutes to actually meet people, find out why they are there, and get to know them a bit. This can be a way of building some sense of relationship even before a newcomer leaves the service.
- *A "Next Step" Event.* Use a teaching series on community or relationships that culminates in a "connection weekend" so that the service theme is integrated with the opportunity to immediately proceed to some other space (lobby, classroom, patio) where a thirty- to sixty-minute experience is created for forming groups or building friendships.
- *Program Tear-Off Form.* Written materials can be designed especially for a connection weekend. If budgets are tight, simply redesign a portion of the existing bulletin or program with a small tear-off section that people can use to express interest in a group. These can be collected during the service. We do not recommend simply saying, "Take time during the service to fill out the form and drop it off on your way out." There are too many steps involved and people forget. During announcements or before a benediction, simply ask people to fill out the form and pass it to an usher. Or ask them to put it in the offering plate. In any case, they need guidance and an opportunity now, while they are thinking about it, to take an action step.

2. Leverage Felt Needs

When people come to your visitor area, meet-the-pastor event, newcomer coffee, or information table, they tend to have needs that fall into one of five categories. It is vital that, as appropriate and without being pushy, you gather information so someone can follow up with the person. Email address and phone numbers are essential these days. Folks might be in a bit of a hurry or have an obligation for lunch or to visit family and have only a few minutes to fill out a card. So provide a brief, clear, easy-to-fill-out information card.

Information about the Church

Some people simply want to know more about the church, the ministries represented, church beliefs, or how to find a certain class. Not everyone wants a long conversation or presentation. Many simply want to know how and where to access the information they seek. Here are three means of providing what they want.

1. *Written Materials.* Don't overwhelm them by providing three dozen brochures about all the ministries, classes, and serving opportunities available. For newcomers, give them only the core information, and keep it brief and clear.
2. *Website.* If possible, have a terminal available where people can go online and discover more about your ministry. Be sure that the church website is current, clear, and accurate.
3. *Conversation.* Some people want to talk and need someone who can listen attentively. You can have a separate guest area, or simply have people available after services to sit and chat with folks.

Care or Crisis

Some of your visitors desperately need help. Coming to your church might be a last resort in their minds. Will you be able to respond? Most of the time these people need to talk with someone who is trained to listen to hurting people. Talking to a pastor or counselor or loving volunteer will help them get direction, receive prayer, and find hope for addressing the need.

Depending on the size of church, the number of visitors, and the economic climate in the surrounding community, you might need people with varying levels of expertise. We suggest that churches have a strategic meeting with people in the church or in the community who are in the helping professions. Together you can formulate a strategy for assessing a situation and responding appropriately. Nurses, counselors, social workers, care agencies, lawyers, doctors, and financial counselors would be primary candidates for this gathering.

Spiritual Questions

Naturally, there will be people who want to discuss spiritual questions. Some of these require prayer, and a prayer team or room is a wonderful ministry to have on-site around services.

Others have theological or doctrinal issues to discuss, have questions about the Sunday message or a midweek class, or simply need to talk about spiritual life concerns. Do you have people who are equipped to handle these questions? Can you point people to an upcoming class, meeting, or another person where they can have dialogue about the questions?

Some churches often have "drop-in" seeker groups after services. People can literally walk out of the service, down the hall, and get into a small group discussion for thirty to forty minutes. Trained group leaders help people connect with each other and find a safe place to investigate what the Bible teaches about Jesus and the faith. Some of these become ongoing groups while others have new people coming each week.

Relational Hunger

"I've been coming for a few weeks and want to get connected. Is there a way I can meet some people and begin to get plugged in here?" People who are ready for a group or looking for some new friends usually express some version of these words. Young singles often have a built-in vehicle in churches (a singles group, classes, events) but often couples, divorced folks, and older singles do not have a clear pathway to community.

An ongoing class or gathering in a home provides a great next step for people, and churches should follow up with this desire and offer to take them there. Volunteers should be prepared to walk someone to a class or a newcomer lunch. Follow-up phone calls or emails also ensure that people make progress as they seek to engage with the church.

Serving Opportunities

Thankfully, some people want to get involved in service activities, knowing this is their pathway to meeting people and connecting to the church. Volunteering in children's ministry or the choir, helping the poor, or participating in a "work day" at the church can help to connect people. Don't simply focus on the project; find ways to connect the unconnected who show up and volunteer. Work groups and teams can easily become places of community life for many.

Maximize Your Opportunities

What are our greatest opportunities in the next few months to leverage felt needs as an entry point to small group life?

What are our next steps to make the most of these opportunities?

3. Leverage Medium-Sized Events

Most churches have a full calendar of events. For many churches, a too-full calendar means that events should be evaluated in light of available resources, clarity of mission, and optimal allocation of a leader's time. When properly utilized, though, events can facilitate a connection strategy. Events must be strategically planned, and those who lead them must understand the purpose of the gathering, especially related to connecting new people.

Guidelines for Effective Medium-Sized Events

- *Select a team leader—the right one.* You need someone with administrative and organizational gifts or experience. It is absolutely essential that they are not the kind of person who has to do it all themselves or have the spotlight. This is a team builder who cares about team success.

- *Identify a clear goal: How will you know when you are successful?* Is success simply, "How many people were at the event?" or "How much money did we raise?" or "How many blankets did we collect?" Or is there a relational definition? For example:

  How many new people attended?
  Did we get information to follow up with them?
  How many potential leaders did we meet at this event?

- *Foster accountability for results: Who is responsible for success?* When you know the goal, you can measure outcomes and weigh the true success of the event. The team leader should be able to explain what did and did not work and suggest a process for improvement if such an event is going to be held again. The leader should also identify what can be celebrated about the event.

- *Select a quality leadership team: Share the ministry with people who understand the goal.* Consider the gifts and talents needed before you select the team. The mission determines the team. Who can help with administration, food preparation, group facilitation, marketing, content development, or whatever needs to be done? Choose wisely. Do the people have a heart for this event and how it helps get the mission done? Do they care about people more than logistics?

- *Design a follow-through strategy: What will happen after the event is over?* How will you use the information you gathered to connect people? Who will lead the follow-up efforts? How will you connect with people who expressed interest in a group at the event—by email, phone team, personal conversations? What if people are hard to contact afterward? What happens next? Doing a full debrief of the event—the highs and lows—is a learning experience and provides opportunities to celebrate what God did at the event.

Medium-Sized Events ...

Are not the ultimate stopping place for connection; they are a means to an end. That does not mean genuine friendships cannot develop at an event. It means that the event is a launching point, not an end.

Are a means of connecting people to a group or process. The energy and fun of an event can be a great first step toward group life.

PROCESS TIME

Poke Holes in the Buckets

Which medium-sized events do we currently do that can be repurposed into connection opportunities?

4. Leverage Group Life

The final area to address as you design a robust connection strategy is group life. A one-size-fits-all approach to groups will not accommodate the variety of spiritual needs and levels of maturity represented in the congregation. You must expand the range of group possibilities.

Chapter 6 is dedicated to this topic; it deserves its own chapter because it will be the springboard to an unending source of fertile group growth, leadership opportunity, and life change.

GROUP VARIETY

Expanding Group Life to Foster Spiritual Growth

KEY QUESTION

Do we have a broad array of groups to meet a broad range of needs?

"If two people wave to each other in the parking lot, you call that a small group meeting." Those words echo in our ears many years after they were spoken. The comment was expressed too often and not so humorously at times. Maybe you have been chided in a similar fashion.

Beneath the surface, however, the snide comment exposes a much-neglected principle of group life. How clear are you on what constitutes a viable group? Are you clear with your definition of group life, including how it is designed to help people connect, care for others, and grow in Christ? Does your definition—or at least your regular banter from the pulpit or in church hallways—highlight group attendance, new members, and how many attended the retreat? If so, you might be giving the impression you care more about numbers than people, more about group gains than personal spiritual growth.

We often have pure intentions, but others may wonder about our aims, especially if we're not clear about what really counts.

Making disciples in a local church context is what counts. A small group serves as the means to that end. Like Jesus, we want to turn a ragtag band into disciples. Defining what counts begins with describing how your church will make disciples.

DEFINING DISCIPLE-MAKING

What if someone stops you after the next church service you attend and poses a simple question, "So what is a small group, anyway?" Perhaps they heard an announcement for groups, or heard the pastor encourage them to join one as a way of applying the main point of the sermon. They honestly want to know and suspect you can answer. Having never been in a small group, they feel quite ignorant about what seems commonplace in your church.

The next words out of your mouth may determine whether they embark on the path to spiritual development or decide they have better things to do with their time. In fact, you can tell they do not have time to hear a lecture or sales speech about community. A brief compelling description is all that will do.

PROCESS TIME

Defining Disciple-Making in Your Church

In two or three sentences, what is your current description of a small group? Include details on leadership, group size, and frequency of meetings.

If you want to run an intriguing experiment, pose the foregoing scenario to your church's senior leadership team or to a department gathering where expanding their ministry is high on the agenda. Hearing everyone's individual definitions should prove telling.

Fostering spiritual growth in small groups starts with clarifying your church's vision for community. Varying the intensity of available group experiences follows next. Once these keys are in place, churches can then expand group variety.

KEY 1: BE CLEAR IN YOUR DEFINITIONS

Every church will need to establish multiple group life definitions and then apply each one appropriately. The first defines the leadership's understanding of group life; the second provides a public definition; the third deals with strategy; the fourth addresses how past experiences with group life influence the current definitions; and the last is a group's self-definition. Once each definition is unambiguous and can be employed effectively for the purpose intended, everyone can remain fixed on the surpassing goal of reproducing Christ in disciples' lives.

Leadership Definition

First is a definition used by church leaders to declare their purpose for groups. What will your church count? What matters to those who hired you? A small group in your church could be defined as something like "a group of four to twelve people who meet at least twice each month with a leader who can help them to intentionally pursue full devotion to Christ." Such a description compels everyone to expect an identified leader, a semi-monthly rhythm, a focused spiritual aim, and some boundary on group size.

Is it the right definition? That is for you to decide in your church setting. You may have one you find workable for a few years but then decide to revise. The goal is to declare what success looks like in your small group ministry.

Never be legalistic with this definition. Allow exceptions to the specifications of your definition. At the occasional monthly group meeting strive to attain most of your objectives, but be flexible, allowing within your system, for example, an entry-level gathering for community rookies to feature a brief devotional as its curriculum instead of an intense Bible study. The exceptions shouldn't take over as the rule, but you should be flexible enough that you can provide for everyone the kind of experience that will most likely lead to the optimal discipleship experience in your setting.

A description is very helpful for ministry staff and volunteers whatever their age, need, affinity, or geographic focus. They all should know what groups are supposed to be within their arena, so everyone can work together to build a church of life-changing community.

Public Definition

In addition to the leadership's definition of small groups, there is a public definition: How will leaders describe the small group ministry to the congregation? The public definition should be more akin to a motto, something like "a small group is a community where nobody stands alone." Church leaders rarely have an occasion to state the entire leadership definition, let alone remember it, but that is fine, since that is not its purpose.

The measure of the public description is how effectively it unifies your church around groups and acts as a magnet for unconnected people. More than a slogan, but less than a speech, the public definition needs to quickly and accurately depict what the church envisions.

Be careful with what it implies. If the recurring phrase is "doing life together deeply," it might promise more to people than most groups can deliver. Accompany it with frequent illustrations of communities that take amazing vacations, endure incredible crises, and complete intense, lengthy, and graduate-level curricula, and a sure by-product will be disappointed group members who wonder what is wrong with their group.

A better alternative could be something like, "a place to connect and grow." Every group can deliver on that promise. It concisely summarizes the main endeavor for all little communities. It is expansive enough to include a wide range of experiences, while sufficiently incisive to make it more than a passing greeting. If it seems to catch on with everyone in your church, from senior pastor to occasional attendee, the public definition is working.

Strategic Definition

The third type of definition you'll need for your small group ministry is a strategic definition: What is the core mission behind every small group? This is the more elaborate version of the leadership's description, designed to act as true north on the community compass. It aids ministry leaders in sticking with the plot, while embedding in small group leaders the essence of their purpose.

In our experience, this definition should encompass four essential elements:

1. Assign a *leader* deployed by the church to shepherd a flock. There is no such thing as a leaderless group, a rotating shepherd. Such groups exist but rarely produce the kind of connection, care, and discipleship that a trained, approved leader provides. If you are building a church of life-changing small groups, it will be founded on empowered shepherds who band together to transform both your church and individuals' lives.

2. Facilitate people *connecting* with each other. The leader becomes the anchor to which others attach, and by attaching they become identified with their small group. This connection produces a sense that they truly have a church home. If someone asks the group member about their church, they will talk as much about the friends they

have made in community as the teaching, worship, or programs. The covenant they have with each other and the relational tie they build defines their experience in the church.

3. Create an environment for *giving and receiving care* — a setting of *mutual* care, where the whole group shows up for the person in need. Care requires give and take, people showing up for each other in the joys and difficulties of their lives. Building these kinds of groups decentralizes pastoral ministry and reinforces the priesthood of all believers, so that the "one anothers" of Scripture become routine over time.

4. Focus on taking people just *the next step*. When churches talk about discipleship, many small group leaders feel like failures if they can't move people from heathen to missionary in less than two years. Most of us, however, have not developed in our faith in that manner; rather, our growth has resulted from many groups varying in nature. Remind leaders that God is at work, and that they are to come alongside him, joining in his effort. It is helpful to define progress as developing people according to a church strategy (such as the five Gs discussed earlier).

Pause to ponder these elements for a moment. If every group is characterized by these four essentials, community can find life in a wide variety of settings, for kids and adults, for women and men, for the broken and mature, for theological study and missional community. A sharp strategic definition opens the door to an incredible array of group experiences that will mature the disciples. Each leader and each group will help disciples take the next step God has for them.

Default Definition

The fourth definition is the default definition. It answers the question, What will inappropriately narrow spiritual growth in community? It addresses the need to guard against one-dimensional discipleship concepts.

Most longstanding churchgoers have had exposure to parachurch small groups, which usually set a high standard for curriculum, frequency, and outcomes, creating the impression that the only group that should count is a high frequency, curriculum-intensive, knowledge-focused Bible study. Often these were experienced on college campuses or in a marketplace setting. These are not bad; they are admirable examples of group learning. But they are not the only setting God uses with people on their journey as disciples.

In the early stages of building a church of life-changing small groups, people will default to a narrow definition based on the historic contexts of their discipleship experiences. As you explain the church's theology of community, describe how a point leader, coaches, and small group leaders will turn vision into reality, and then introduce everyone to your leadership, public, and strategic definitions, your congregation will become comfortable with a broader array of group-based spiritual development alternatives.

At least for a season they'll be content.

Pockets of staff or ministry leaders may remain influenced by previous group experiences and bring about subtle but possibly debilitating shifts. The "mom's play groups" are jettisoned in favor of ladies' Bible studies. Entry-level groups are neglected in favor of discipleship groups, and serving groups are "reduced" to a focus on the task while members are urged to "do relationships in another ministry."

The shift toward a narrower concept of what counts as a group is inevitable. You will have to discern and confront such narrowing tendencies and reinforce the broader landscape of groups for building community.

Group Definition

Last is the definition each group provides for itself: What is your purpose as a small group? This may be the characterization that matters most to the average church attendee. Every one of them comes to their group with expectations they anticipate the community will fulfill. Likewise, the group leader initiates with intentions about what the group will be. If both expectations and intentions remain unspoken, all participants may miss an essential definition.

For this reason we encourage every group to create a covenant that defines the anticipated group experience for everyone involved. A covenant could be expressed as an equation like this:

Intentions + Expectations = Covenant

Another phrase for this, aptly described in *Making Small Groups Work* by Cloud and Townsend, is "ground rules." Ground rules simply express the *collective* intentions and expectations all participants bring to the table.

The most important dynamic to understand is that every group has a covenant, whether stated or not! Problems are unavoidable in groups where ground rules go unstated. Disappointment, colliding visions, and divergent group definitions create trouble. Bypassing the covenant process creates far more problems. For more on this process for your groups' leaders, you can consult not only the *Making Small Groups Work* DVD, but also this handbook's sister guide, *Leading Life-Changing Small Groups.*

Be broad with your leadership, public, and strategic definitions, and narrow with individual group definitions. Encourage precision at the individual community level.

KEY 2: VARY THE INTENSITY OF GROUP EXPERIENCE AND COMMITMENT

As you sharpen the concept of disciple-making in your church by understanding leadership, public, strategic, default, and group definitions, you will provide a foundation for another key in expanding the range of group experiences: varying the intensity of group experience and commitment. In addition to establishing the definitions discussed above, you should analyze the intensity of existing and needed group life in your church.

To direct your thinking about the possible breadth of group experience and commitment, consider the framework in the following table. It begins in the upper left, increasing the intensity at each lower box. Associated with each intensity level is increasing frequency of meeting and group experiences. You can start to think of some examples of different groups you've seen or participated in that fit the category.

Purpose	Meetings per month	Experiences	Examples
Connection and Support	1–2	Prayer, Sharing, and Serving	
Community and Growth	2–4	Add: Devotional Discussion Relationship Building	
Intentional Development	3–4	Add: Bible Study Curriculum	
Leadership and Ministry Development	4+	Add: Spiritual Disciplines Skills and Training	

To expand your thinking about the kinds of groups that might fit each intensity level, here is the identical framework with some examples provided. Further description of each example follows the table.

Purpose	Meetings per month	Experience	Examples
Connection and Support	1–2	Prayer, Sharing, and Serving	Serving Small Groups Community Groups "50/50" Groups
Community and Growth	2–4	Add: Devotional Discussion Relationship Building	*Our Daily Bread* Reading Leader Devotional Sharing Message-Based Groups
Intentional Development	3–4	Add: Bible Study Curriculum	Bible Studies Discipleship Groups Seeker Small Groups
Leadership and Ministry Development	4+	Add: Spiritual Disciplines Skills and Training	Spiritual Formation Groups Neighborhood Groups Turbo Groups

Serving Small Groups. A set of volunteers organized into a serving group, who take some time to cluster, share needs, pray for each other, and perform their tasks together. Could involve ushering, traffic control, maintenance, setup, groundskeeping.

Community Groups. An entry level social (i.e. dessert and coffee required!) gathering in a host's home that allows attendees a regular place to see friends, come under the guidance of a leader, and share and pray for mutual concerns.

"50/50" Groups. Similar to a community group, but organized so a whole church is assigned a spot to meet semi-monthly (first and third Sunday afternoon, for example) for a one-hour sharing (50 percent) and praying (50 percent) experience.

Our Daily Bread Reading. Our Daily Bread is a time-tested devotional that the leader of a serving community could use to add a moment of reflection to a current volunteer group's meeting, simply reading the day's entry before serving together.

Leader Devotional Sharing. "The best curriculum for every group is the leader's life," Dan Webster has taught. Any leader who has a vital daily solitude experience can use his journey with God by sharing it with a community group.

Message-Based Groups. A simple format for lower intensity settings using three simple discussion questions groups use to debrief a weekend message. It reinforces service attendance, applies sermons, and permits pastors to hand off responsibilities to leaders.

Bible Studies. Main Street for group life, the vehicle through which communities can deepen in grace and truth. Whether facilitated by a written curriculum or a leader skilled at inductive discussions, the Bible is useful in every way (2 Timothy 3:16).

Discipleship Groups. Similar to a Bible study, can focus on specific and methodical development of an individual's character and spiritual practices, particularly through a fixed season of study with a group.

Seeker Small Groups. Formed to help people investigate God, can be lower intensity, but will tackle serious issues requiring intensive study and focus on deep issues of the faith.

Spiritual Formation Groups. Groups that allow for making connections, sharing spiritual practices, and mutual mentoring, therefore increasing intensity. In addition to Bible study and discipleship, these communities fit the "doing life deeply together" description.

Neighborhood Groups. Sometimes organized to be a less extreme group experience, but geographic proximity can dramatically deepen life-on-life connection due to the daily rhythm it introduces.

Turbo Groups. Designed to accelerate the development of a new generation of small group leaders. Uniquely intense due to the desire to give apprentices accelerated development.

When building a church of life-changing small groups, one of the key jobs of church leadership is to constantly broaden the array of small group options through varied intensity. First timers are going to be reluctant to make a commitment to a once-per-week two-hour Bible study. But if someone has a good experience at one intensity level, they will vote for more, increasing the intensity of their experience as they mature.

The level of commitment and intensity that people need can vary as they go through the seasons of life. If their group participation demands too great a time commitment when life requires a different rhythm, people are likely to opt out completely. To address this, churches should add low-intensity, low-commitment groups to help people connect. God can still work in their life, though, even in a less intensive group experience and commitment.

You cannot allow over-the-fence judgment to deem one intensity or commitment level better than the other; they merely differ. It is not about strict categorization; it is about a continuum of connection, about meeting people at their point of readiness for fruitful community.

PROCESS TIME

Varying Group Intensity

What percentage of groups does your church have in each category? Take a moment to fill in your own examples based on your ministry, or use this tool to engage a leadership team or ministry department.

Purpose	Meetings per month	Experiences	Examples
Connection and Support	1–2	Prayer, Sharing, and Serving	
Community and Growth	2–4	Add: Devotional Discussion Relationship Building	
Intentional Development	3–4	Add: Bible Study Curriculum	
Leadership and Ministry Development	4+	Add: Spiritual Disciplines Skills and Training	

KEY 3: EXPAND THE OPPORTUNITIES

Intensity variation is a helpful way to evaluate the diversity of community. Create identifiable open doors unconnected individuals can use to identify how and where they are willing to make their move toward a group.

You've seen some examples in the prior section. They barely scratch the surface of an endless array of groups, teams, communities, and relationships. Your imagination, experimentation, and localized effectiveness are the only limits.

Here is a sampling from which you can work.

Possible Kinds of Groups/Connections

1. *Affinity.* What do we have in common that creates a natural point of contact and connection?

   Interest-Based (Medical, Computer, Pilots, Seekers)
   Age-Based (Children, Youth, Gen-X, Seniors)
   Stage-Based (Couples, Newly Married, Family)

2. *Seeker* (Spiritual Discovery, Alpha, Neighborhood Bible Studies). What questions do we have about the faith and how can we create a learning experience for like-minded explorers?
3. *Task-Based or Serving-Focused* (Ushers, Work Teams, Choir, Food Pantry). How can we leverage something we are doing to create biblical community?
4. *Care-Based* (Divorce/Grief Recovery, Job Loss). What pain do we share that draws us together, and how can we build a community that encourages and supports us in the process?
5. *Geographical.* How do we capitalize on where we live or where we work or where we go to school in order to launch some groups?

Each of these types of groups is filled with possibilities for those who are creative and willing to explore new ways of doing group life.

PROCESS TIME

What Kinds of Groups Can We Create?

How will you create a wider range of group experiences in order to connect a wider range of people who need support, encouragement, and direction for moving ahead in their relationship with God and others?

Chapter 7

OPEN GROUPS

Reproducing Leaders and Groups

Two major factors must be addressed in order to multiply the ministry of group life throughout the church: developing an open group mindset and creating strategies for multiplying group life. Open groups are places where people can connect to an existing community; multiplying group life requires a continual flow of new leaders and the launching of new groups.

DEVELOP AN OPEN GROUP MINDSET

The issue of group multiplication continues to inspire vigorous debate at times. A key factor in multiplying a group is growing the group by adding new people. How do we add people? Do we have to add people? How often do we connect new folks to the group? What about our ever-deepening relationships? Will newcomers threaten those relationships? Will we sacrifice depth for breadth?

Questions and concerns are legitimate, though some are motivated more by fear than by the desire to create a workable strategy. An open group is not a group where people run in and out each week, where there is no commitment, where attendance at meetings does not matter, or where building relationships takes a back seat to growing the numbers.

Guiding the ministry toward a vision for growth and expansion requires leadership and never allows us to settle for the idea that we have enough groups or enough people in groups. As a church grows, the number of groups must grow as well. The question is not, Should we open our group to new people? Rather, the question is, Should we open our *minds and hearts* to new people?

Here are some guidelines for creating and maintaining an open group mindset where group members actively seek God's will and pursue opportunities for growth.

Cast a Courageous Vision

Coaches, leaders, and group members must come to grips with the reality that some people have no community life, no small group of people with whom to do life together. Vision flows from identifying the problem—lonely people are seeking a community—and framing a solution.

"A place where no one stands alone" is a visionary reminder of the kind of church we want to become. The best way to cast vision is to tell compelling stories that illustrate an open group mindset. When groups hear stories of people who finally got connected, or when they hear stories of people feeling disconnected and subsequently leaving the church, their hearts are moved.

Our wives have experienced such openness—the kind that changes lives and impacts groups forever. When the Robinsons had young children, Lynn was invited to a mom's group—a play group for kids—where she could connect and share life with other moms facing similar challenges. The group was instrumental in Lynn's spiritual journey and growth in Christ. She met her best friend the first day she attended it, and their ministry together has touched many other women and couples.

Imagine the group saying to Lynn, "It is a shame you struggle just like we do—we sure hope some people invite you into a group somewhere. Ours is just not open right now. We really like ours just the way it is."

What if several years ago Gail Donahue had said no to three non-Christians who wanted to be in her small group? They were halfway through Romans (a light, easy read—not!) with a curriculum designed to help believers—not seekers—understand their faith. She could have said, "Well, the group is just not designed for you." Like Lynn's group, though, she had an open group mindset, a willingness to connect people even if it is not in the plan.

She said yes. One year later all three had received Christ and remain faithful followers today. What if ... what if these groups had embraced a closed group mindset?

Consider Group Size

Group size is also a determining factor when it comes to adding members. Members of groups with ten or more people begin to feel the tension. Each person wants to share a story, reflect on Scripture, pray and be prayed for, yet there is less time for each person as the group grows in number.

Once a group reaches twelve or more it is time to begin thinking about subgrouping strategies, at least for a portion of a meeting. The group can grow larger—up to twenty or more—but more people necessitates more structure. A group of three people meeting for lunch to pray and encourage each other requires no real leader. A group of twelve requires more structure, meeting preparation, and facilitation to make sure the group process keeps working for everyone.

If your group has ten or more people, your focus should be leadership identification and development (to multiply groups you need more leaders). If your group has fewer than ten, you have room for two or three new members. If you use a large group/small group strategy, you can accommodate several more people.

Model the Open Chair

Group leaders (and point leaders who are leading their own group) must model the values and practices of the group they lead. If we want people to pray, we pray. If we desire our group members to serve the poor, we serve the poor.

The "open chair" concept is no different. Encouraged by cell church advocates and by group life experts for some time, the open chair is an image that communicates a spirit of welcome. Some groups actually place an open chair in the circle during meetings to remind group members that we have room for more.

If members are not readily inviting friends, then leaders must take the lead. We have seen the difference it makes when we build relationships and invite people into community. It inspires other members, brings new life to the group, and increases the leader's credibility.

Make Relationships the Key Factor

While it is great that some groups can invite complete strangers unannounced to meetings, many leaders and groups find this awkward. Here is a process most groups can use for inviting people to a group.

- *Build a relationship with a prospective member.* Reach out to people you meet in classes, at services, at work, or in the community where you live. Get to know them, care about them, and think of their needs and interests (not your agenda: "I am going to get this guy in our group if it kills me!").
- *Connect them socially with other group members.* Connect new friends with group members as you go about the week. Sit together at services, have dinner, enjoy a soccer match together. Help the new person to connect with other group members.
- *Invite them to a small group meeting.* Finally, invite them to a meeting.

Make sure everyone knows he/she is coming, spend time building the relationship, tell some group stories, enjoy some food, laugh, pray, and have a brief discussion. It will likely take a few meetings until a new person feels comfortable. The key here is "relationship first, group meeting second."

PROCESS TIME

Open Group Mindset

How will we create an open group mindset? Where do we need to focus our energy?

Cast a Courageous Vision
Consider Group Size
Model the Open Chair
Build Relationships

STRATEGIES FOR MULTIPLYING GROUP LIFE

A thriving and growing group ministry requires the identification of new leaders and the utilization of creative strategies for launching new groups. Each of the strategies below has served us over the years—some have been used often, others less so.

- Identifying and Developing Apprentice Leaders
- Launching Turbo Groups
- Leveraging Medium-Sized Groups
- Birthing New Groups
- Experimenting with Campaigns and Seasonal Groups

1. Identify and Develop Apprentice Leaders: Passing the Leadership Baton

What Do You Look For?

The best apprentices may not look like group leaders. They have leadership potential but still have some growing to do. People often ask us, "So what specifically are you looking for in an apprentice?"

Do not look for leaders; look for people—there are more of them! If you have a set idea of what a leader should look like, you are probably overlooking many viable candidates. When looking for leaders, people tend to look for those who are like themselves or who are like successful leaders they admire. God intends different kinds of leaders for different kinds of groups. In a small group ministry, look for apprentices who have the right raw material (your church will have to decide just how "raw" you can tolerate). Remember, if they were ready to lead they would not need to serve as apprentices.

The right people should be eager to learn, humble enough to listen and be trained, and committed to the vision of group life in the church.

Where Do You Find Them?

Potential leaders exist wherever there are people gathering regularly. The best place to look is in the group you lead. Have you overlooked someone quiet or shy? Have you missed a leadership candidate in your group because you are too busy leading to be thinking about the next leader?

Meet people in classes you take, at social activities, churchwide events, and celebrations, and at serving opportunities.

What Are the Responsibilities of an Apprentice?

1. *Love* the group members. Even though an apprentice is going to leave and lead their own group some day they can still deeply love the people in this group now.
2. *Learn* from the leader how to lead a group, pray with people, handle conflict, lead discussions, and organize a meeting. Leaders should debrief each meeting with the apprentice and share ideas, offer feedback, and consider leadership opportunities for the next meeting. Groups are more than meetings, so the leader and apprentice should discuss other aspects of group life between meetings.
3. *Lead* some part of the meeting or entire meetings. Apprentices grow and learn by doing what the leader does (and then receiving feedback).
4. *Look* for potential ministry partners and group members. The apprentice is going to be a leader and needs an apprentice as well as some new members.

2. Launch Turbo Groups: Gathering an All-Apprentice Community

You can launch several groups at once by training several leaders together in a turbo group—a group filled with apprentices.

The objective behind the turbo experience is twofold: (1) to become a real, authentic small group, and (2) to learn the skills and process of group leadership. It is not designed to be simply a "leadership training" group, because these apprentices will ultimately lead regular groups (not leadership training groups). Their experience in the turbo group therefore must be as close as possible to real group life.

The group should follow a rhythm that alternates between small group activity and time for processing the leadership implications of what is happening. At the end of each meeting, participants should debrief, receive feedback, and plan the next gathering. The leaders should discuss what has been learned and provide specific coaching to those who had leadership roles during the meeting. Rotate leaders each week so everyone gets a chance to lead and gain valuable feedback about their leadership. Start by assigning parts of the meeting (like prayer time or the discussion) to one or more people. Each person should lead an entire meeting.

Building relationships (even though the group may only last a few months) and investing in one another's lives are important aspects of the turbo group. Use five to ten minutes each session for a group member to tell their life story (abbreviated LS in the table on page 163). It does not have to cover the events of their entire life, but should offer an overview of their journey. Important dates, events, relationships, jobs, education, and personal hobbies or dreams are typically discussed. Allow a few minutes for group members to ask questions.

The head of the turbo group models the kind of group life they want these leaders to emulate when they have their own groups.

On page 163 is a sample turbo group format. Turbo groups have no set curriculum, because each group varies in the maturity of the apprentices and the group experience they have had. The key is to do your best to create an authentic small group while developing leaders.

3. Leverage Medium-Sized Groups: Finding Groups in a Group

One way to start a group is to find a potential leader, train them, and help them build relationships and then launch a group. Instead of the "find a leader, build a community" approach, you can reverse the order. First, build a community; then discover the leaders. That is why we use medium-sized group gatherings (MSGs).

Here are some general guidelines for MSGs:

- *Size*: Fifteen to fifty people
- *Location*: A classroom at church, an activity room in an apartment complex, or a home
- *Time*: About ninety minutes for meetings
- *Leadership*: Two to four hosts/leaders who can create a strong relational dynamic and a warm, inviting environment
- *Leader Qualifications*: Should meet your baseline requirements, but look for people who have hospitality gifts, are relationally savvy, and can identify or lead emerging leaders

SAMPLE TURBO GROUP MEETING FORMAT

Each meeting should last about ninety minutes
Each meeting should contain the following components:

- Experiential learning
- Knowledge/teaching by the main leader
- Evaluation of development by the main leader
- Specific skills practiced and taught
- Communication of vision for small groups, shepherding, church of groups, etc.

Meeting	Content
1	Acquaintance/Mission/Vision/Values/Social
2	Vision/Life Stories (LS — do 1 each meeting)/Prayer
3	Vision/Leadership/Shepherding/LS
4	Using the Open Chair (actually add a newcomer here)/LS
5	Leading a Bible Discussion (two people lead each meeting)/LS
6*	Prayer/Worship in Groups/Subgroup/LS
7	Pastoral Care — Meeting Needs/LS
8	Apprentice ID and Development
9	Conflict Management
10	Planning and Designing a Meeting
11	Launching — Prepare
12	Evaluate and Commissioning (allow extra time for this)

*If possible, have a half-day or all-day retreat/getaway before meeting 6 to speed up the community-building process and to allow everyone to practice some leadership skills. Get a couple more life stories done at meal times.

Note: You may need more than one meeting for each of the above; many turbo groups last from six months to one year. Plan for about nine months with breaks and a retreat.

- *Content*: About ten minutes of teaching content to the entire group, followed by subgrouping into groups of three to five for discussion
- *Format*:

  Ten Minutes: Arrive and socialize; snacks and drinks
  Ten Minutes: Welcome, overview, and teaching (live or DVD)
  Twenty Minutes: Discussion in subgroups; give each group a card with a question or two for discussion; ask them to select a facilitator to make sure they stay on time and everyone gets a chance to talk

Ten Minutes: Prayer in subgroups

Twenty Minutes: large group debrief and shared learning

Ten Minutes: Closing comments, announcements, schedules, etc.

Ten Minutes: Socialize again; people can stay longer but keep to the timing for those with other commitments or babysitters, etc.

- *Structure*: This group is designed so that the hosts/leader team can "float" to the various small groups to make observations, see how things are going, and answer questions.

Over the course of a few meetings the groups will settle in and the rhythm will feel comfortable. Be creative and consider varying the length of segments as you see fit. The MSG team's purpose is to look for leaders. Rotate facilitators and observe who is doing a good job. Ask group members for feedback, as they may be future group leaders.

As the MSG leadership team identifies emerging leaders, ask these folks to arrive early to meet and pray before the others arrive. This can evolve into a leadership development time. As time progresses there are several options:

- *Launch an MSG*. Keep adding people and launch another MSG from this group. For example, if space is getting tight in a group of twenty to thirty, simply ask twelve to fifteen people to become the core of another MSG and launch a new one.
- *Launch small groups from the MSG*. The smaller groups of four to five can begin to add people and then become a regular home group.
- *Hybrid*. Meet one week as an MSG and meet the next week in small groups. The group will create a rhythm that allows for growth and energy (when all are present) while allowing a small group experience for people every other week.

Focus on building quality community and raising leaders. Depending on how things are going, choose one of the strategies above and multiply the ministry. MSGs can be a great tool for relationship building and leadership development at the same time!

You might already have some MSGs—classes, social gatherings, men's or women's fellowships. Think about how you might bring community to them and launch some groups from those gatherings.

4. Launch New Groups: Regenerating New Communities

Leaders who have identified and developed an apprentice, and have grown their group to at least twelve to fourteen people, will be able to launch a new group. Here are the options:

- The apprentice leaves and starts a new group
- The apprentice takes a few existing group members with them and starts a new group
- The leader leaves to start a new group and the apprentice becomes the leader of the original group

Steps to Launching a Group

1. *Cast a vision for launching.* Help people understand the focus of connecting the unconnected who need a community for their growth.
2. *Prepare your group and apprentice.* Spend several weeks praying about the launch and select a date. Allow plenty of time for the group to emotionally prepare for sending some people out or losing a leader. Some may be sad about this. Help them understand this is normal and that you will remain very connected to the new group.
3. *Find new apprentices.* Let's say you plan to launch a new group in three or four months. The apprentice and the leader each need to find apprentices. This allows the new group to launch with a leadership team and the existing group to identify another emerging leader to develop.
4. *Subgroup the members.* In the months leading up to the birth, spend some part of the meeting in subgroups, allowing the apprentice to lead about half the group while the leader guides the other members. Two groups within the larger group begin to form, have an identity of their own, and can begin to invite others to join them.
5. *Celebrate new life/grieve the losses.* When the day arrives, pray over the new group; commission them and bless them. Celebrate, tell stories, and express any sadness that people are leaving the group. To maintain the relationships, we suggest you gather as a large group every other week until it is clear that each group needs to have its own time and process.

5. Experiment with Campaigns and Seasonal Groups: Creating Tastes of Community

Small Group Campaigns

Churchwide campaigns have proven to be effective tools for encouraging people to join a group for the first time. By focusing the entire church on a theme, with an accompanying sermon series by the pastor, groups can have a common experience. DVD teaching or a common curriculum for all groups can provide a sense of synergy and unity. Usually groups last about six weeks, enabling people to take the risk without making a long-term commitment to a given group.

One caution about campaigns: make sure to offer adequate leadership training and have a support structure in place. It is quite common for us to hear, "We launched forty-five groups during a campaign, but now we only have twenty—what happened?" Usually these churches provided no support structure, no coaching, no leadership development, and no real integration of the short-term group experience with ongoing group life.

Seasonal and Short-Term Groups

Seasonal and short-term groups are similar to the campaign idea, but are not necessarily churchwide and linked to a message series from the pastor. These "groups for a season" are often eight- to twelve-week groups, aligned with the school calendar. Churches using this system launch groups in the fall, winter, and spring. Some use the summer as well, while others take a summer break to focus on leadership recruitment for the fall.

Short-term groups should strive to dive in and become a deeply connected group as soon as possible, since there is so little time. Leaders must create a sense of oneness and engagement quickly. We used this process at Willow, created some DVD training for the leaders, chose curriculum, and launched about seventy groups. After the eight-week experience about 80 percent of the groups decided to continue on as small groups. Why was this successful?

First, it was a new approach and many people who had been hesitant to join a group (for whatever the reason) decided that a short-term group was worth the risk (and offered a way out if the group was "weird").

Second, instead of avoiding deep relationships and commitment in such a short-term experience, we decided to do just the opposite. We encouraged and trained the leaders to challenge group members. "Since we only have eight sessions, let's not hold back. We want to share our lives, pray for each other, study Scripture, and really engage in the process of growth. Time is short. Let's make the most of it!"

Third, we chose the curriculum. That allowed the leaders to focus on the process and the people. It kept things simple and streamlined.

———

Regardless of the strategy you choose, chances are it is not a silver bullet that will work every time. Vary your strategies; try new approaches; mix it up. It will spark your creativity, and refreshing approaches will attract different kinds of people to groups.

PROCESS TIME

COMMUNITIES THAT REACH A COMMUNITY

One of our favorite, recurring group life themes has been "Community with a Cause." We used it in meetings, to envision leaders, and at retreats for small-group leaders. It captures both vision and a warning.

"Community with a Cause" offers a *vision* for group life that has the power to touch people in ways that few other ministry strategies can. It meets them at their particular point of need and has more potential for personal touch and flexible response than most other church programs. When a little community remains open to how God might use them, their alignment with God's causes in our world, life by life, has limitless potential for impact.

This vision for community life also stands as a *warning* against what so often inhibits the power of small group ministry: "Community with a Cap." When a group turns inward and loses its missional fervor, the work of the Spirit gets quenched. Helping leaders and their flocks understand the rhythms of regular receptivity, timely inclusion, and effective multiplication will take them on the adventure of their life together.

Only heaven will tell the story of what such a small band of Christ-followers birthed—just like that first small group of guys Jesus unleashed.

Chapter 8

MEASURING PROGRESS

Assessing Your Ministry's Next Steps

When it comes to the number of groups, leaders, participants, and the like, churches can measure their progress in building a life-changing small group ministry. Yet, how do they measure overall ministry strength and weakness, using the concepts from *Building a Life-Changing Small Group Ministry*, in order to know what might be holding back progress, lurking as a barrier to growth, or missing as a leverage point to remarkable results?

KEY QUESTION

What are our next steps to build and grow our small group ministry?

Tracking progress in a small group ministry isn't a precise science. Leaders can analyze their ministries, process the results, and convey them in a way that invites discussion, shares the assessment process, and provides insightful conclusions about the areas requiring most attention. This chapter will guide you through the process by use of an evaluation tool. The Grouplife Assessment is designed to measure and compare various categories of small group ministry to see which is strongest and what areas demand the most attention.

The following section presents numerous questions to ask as you evaluate your small group ministry. Each page is devoted to questions gleaned from the content of *Building a Life-Changing Small Group Ministry*. Based on the key points of the book, you will score your church on the following group life ministry categories:

- Ministry Strategy
- Point Leadership
- Support Structures
- Leadership Development
- Connection Strategy
- Range of Group Experiences
- Multiplying Group Life

Once you have answered questions about each subject, you can add some open-ended comments. The final page allows you to tally your findings and compare the relative strength or weakness for each category.

INSTRUCTIONS FOR COMPLETING THE GROUPLIFE ASSESSMENT

As you complete the succeeding pages, answer each question for the category by placing an "x" in the box based on the following scale:

5 = Usually True
4 = Sometimes True
3 = True or False Equally
2 = Sometimes False
1 = Usually False
0 = Do Not Know

After completing the open-ended narrative questions, it won't take you long to transfer your scores to the summary page. Completing the bottom half of the summary page will provide you "a math moment"—do not be intimidated; it is simple to follow!—so that by totaling the scores and comparing your findings about each category of your small group ministry you will see its strengths, as well as the opportunities to grow group life in your church.

Ministry Strategy						
Description	**Evaluation Score**					
As a congregation we are clear on the purpose of small groups within our ministry.	☐ 5	☐ 4	☐ 3	☐ 2	☐ 1	☐ 0
Church staff members are supportive of small groups even when their roles aren't directly related to the small group ministry.	☐ 5	☐ 4	☐ 3	☐ 2	☐ 1	☐ 0
Small groups are an integral part of each ministry of our church.	☐ 5	☐ 4	☐ 3	☐ 2	☐ 1	☐ 0
Church staff members are intentional about connecting people to small groups in their individual areas.	☐ 5	☐ 4	☐ 3	☐ 2	☐ 1	☐ 0
Every small group leader understands their role in achieving the church's dream for community through small groups.	☐ 5	☐ 4	☐ 3	☐ 2	☐ 1	☐ 0
Everything we do in regard to our small group ministry is evaluated in light of the small group strategy we have communicated to the congregation.	☐ 5	☐ 4	☐ 3	☐ 2	☐ 1	☐ 0

	5	4	3	2	1	0
My church leaders (senior pastor, ministry pastors, directors, and leaders) have a clear picture of what they want the small group ministry to become in the future.	☐	☐	☐	☐	☐	☐
My church's small group strategy is frequently communicated to the congregation.	☐	☐	☐	☐	☐	☐
Our church is clear on our definition of what constitutes an official small group.	☐	☐	☐	☐	☐	☐
Our church values building relationships between people more than developing programs.	☐	☐	☐	☐	☐	☐
Our coaches and staff stay in close contact with groups and group leaders.	☐	☐	☐	☐	☐	☐
The approach to small groups at my church is intentional and well thought out, and integrates well into the vision of our church and its uniqueness.	☐	☐	☐	☐	☐	☐
The different ministries of my church (music, education, counseling, children and youth, senior adult, church administration, small groups, etc.) appear to be united by shared, clear, churchwide small group goals.	☐	☐	☐	☐	☐	☐
The expectations for how our corporate worship and our small group gatherings relate to each other are clearly communicated.	☐	☐	☐	☐	☐	☐
The unique vision of my church, and how small group ministry fits within that vision, is well understood throughout the congregation.	☐	☐	☐	☐	☐	☐
There is significant agreement among small group members, small group leaders, and coaches regarding the role of small groups in the overall ministry and vision of the church.	☐	☐	☐	☐	☐	☐
The leaders of our church are personally involved in a small group.	☐	☐	☐	☐	☐	☐
Leaders of the church are consistent in what they say about the importance of small groups and what they do in their leadership roles.	☐	☐	☐	☐	☐	☐
We rarely lose sight of how our small group ministry connects to our congregation's larger, more comprehensive vision.	☐	☐	☐	☐	☐	☐
Our members believe participation in a small group is just as important as attending worship, Bible study, and stewardship.	☐	☐	☐	☐	☐	☐
It is normal for members to participate in a small group in our church; in fact, it is expected.	☐	☐	☐	☐	☐	☐
Total of Each Score	___5s	___4s	___3s	___2s	___1s	___0s

Point Leadership						
Description	**Evaluation Score**					
Our church has a person — in either a staff or volunteer role — whose one job responsibility is to lead our small group ministry.	☐ 5	☐ 4	☐ 3	☐ 2	☐ 1	☐ 0
The person in charge of our small group ministry — our point leader — regularly (at least annually) evaluates the health of our small group ministry.	☐ 5	☐ 4	☐ 3	☐ 2	☐ 1	☐ 0
Our point leader balances the need for quantity of people in groups with quality of group life.	☐ 5	☐ 4	☐ 3	☐ 2	☐ 1	☐ 0
Our point leader continuously seeks new ways and approaches to improve our small group ministry.	☐ 5	☐ 4	☐ 3	☐ 2	☐ 1	☐ 0
Our point leader regularly and effectively communicates the importance of small groups to the church.	☐ 5	☐ 4	☐ 3	☐ 2	☐ 1	☐ 0
Our point leader focuses our church on the future vision for our small group ministry.	☐ 5	☐ 4	☐ 3	☐ 2	☐ 1	☐ 0
Our point leader is well suited for his or her position, exhibiting a passion for small groups and knowledge of how to lead a small group ministry.	☐ 5	☐ 4	☐ 3	☐ 2	☐ 1	☐ 0
Our point leader ensures that group leaders are interviewed and positioned to lead the group best suited to their gifts and abilities.	☐ 5	☐ 4	☐ 3	☐ 2	☐ 1	☐ 0
Our point leader is effective at solving strategic problems that affect the entire small group ministry and the life of the church.	☐ 5	☐ 4	☐ 3	☐ 2	☐ 1	☐ 0
Our point leader is a part of the top leadership in our church and is positioned to significantly contribute to building a structure that supports small groups.	☐ 5	☐ 4	☐ 3	☐ 2	☐ 1	☐ 0
The point leader has a job description that provides clear expectations and is a good basis for performance appraisal.	☐ 5	☐ 4	☐ 3	☐ 2	☐ 1	☐ 0
While supportive, the point leader allows small group leaders and small groups to solve their own problems; they don't take over the role of the small group leader when issues arise.	☐ 5	☐ 4	☐ 3	☐ 2	☐ 1	☐ 0
Total of Each Score	___5s	___4s	___3s	___2s	___1s	___0s

Support Structures

Description	Evaluation Score					
Our small group ministry has defined a volunteer role — a "coach" — who provides support and direction for our small group leaders.	☐ 5	☐ 4	☐ 3	☐ 2	☐ 1	☐ 0
Before becoming coaches, our coaches have led small groups.	☐ 5	☐ 4	☐ 3	☐ 2	☐ 1	☐ 0
Our coaches meet with the leaders they serve on a regular basis (every four to six weeks).	☐ 5	☐ 4	☐ 3	☐ 2	☐ 1	☐ 0
Most of our small group leaders welcome the care and nurture of their coaches.	☐ 5	☐ 4	☐ 3	☐ 2	☐ 1	☐ 0
Our coaches are an excellent resource to our small group leaders.	☐ 5	☐ 4	☐ 3	☐ 2	☐ 1	☐ 0
Our coaches are very skilled in developing personal relationships with the small group leaders they serve.	☐ 5	☐ 4	☐ 3	☐ 2	☐ 1	☐ 0
Our coaches do a good job of identifying and developing new coaches.	☐ 5	☐ 4	☐ 3	☐ 2	☐ 1	☐ 0
Our coaches understand their role and responsibilities.	☐ 5	☐ 4	☐ 3	☐ 2	☐ 1	☐ 0
Our ministry provides ongoing training for our coaches.	☐ 5	☐ 4	☐ 3	☐ 2	☐ 1	☐ 0
Our small group leaders look to coaches rather than the church staff for leadership and care.	☐ 5	☐ 4	☐ 3	☐ 2	☐ 1	☐ 0
Our small group ministry holds the coaching role in high regard.	☐ 5	☐ 4	☐ 3	☐ 2	☐ 1	☐ 0
Our small group ministry provides as much support to coaches as it does to group leaders.	☐ 5	☐ 4	☐ 3	☐ 2	☐ 1	☐ 0
When our small group leaders encounter problems, they see their coach as a resource for dealing with group-related issues.	☐ 5	☐ 4	☐ 3	☐ 2	☐ 1	☐ 0
Within our small group ministry, a volunteer coach is responsible for the care of no more than five small group leaders.	☐ 5	☐ 4	☐ 3	☐ 2	☐ 1	☐ 0
Total of Each Score	___5s	___4s	___3s	___2s	___1s	___0s

Leadership Development

Description	Evaluation Score					
Apprentice leaders (individuals training to become group leaders) are placed as leaders of their own groups only when they are ready, not just to satisfy a need for a new group leader.	☐ 5	☐ 4	☐ 3	☐ 2	☐ 1	☐ 0
Helping a person discover or identify his or her giftedness is an intentional aspect of our approach to small group leadership development.	☐ 5	☐ 4	☐ 3	☐ 2	☐ 1	☐ 0
Volunteer leadership is a frequent topic of sermons and/or teaching at our church.	☐ 5	☐ 4	☐ 3	☐ 2	☐ 1	☐ 0
My church gives a great deal of attention to the selection of future small group leaders.	☐ 5	☐ 4	☐ 3	☐ 2	☐ 1	☐ 0
Our current small group leaders willingly and intentionally delegate leadership tasks and responsibilities to apprentice leaders as they are developing.	☐ 5	☐ 4	☐ 3	☐ 2	☐ 1	☐ 0
Our small group leaders model the kind of life I'd like to live.	☐ 5	☐ 4	☐ 3	☐ 2	☐ 1	☐ 0
The path from apprentice to small group leader is well defined.	☐ 5	☐ 4	☐ 3	☐ 2	☐ 1	☐ 0
The senior leaders in my congregation — senior pastor, staff, and volunteers — invest time and energy in the growth and development of emerging small group leaders.	☐ 5	☐ 4	☐ 3	☐ 2	☐ 1	☐ 0
There are enough emerging leaders in my church to meet the demands of our small group ministry.	☐ 5	☐ 4	☐ 3	☐ 2	☐ 1	☐ 0
We make clear a distinction between those who assist group leaders administratively (scheduling room setup, organizing, ordering materials, etc.) and apprentice leaders.	☐ 5	☐ 4	☐ 3	☐ 2	☐ 1	☐ 0
We use numerous strategies to identify future small group leaders such as conducting spiritual gifts seminars, observing people during special events, interviewing newcomers, interacting personally, and delegating challenging assignments.	☐ 5	☐ 4	☐ 3	☐ 2	☐ 1	☐ 0
Total of Each Score	___5s	___4s	___3s	___2s	___1s	___0s

Connection Strategy

Description	Evaluation Score					
Newcomers who indicate interest in our church are likely to be contacted within three days of their participation in a church-related activity.	☐ 5	☐ 4	☐ 3	☐ 2	☐ 1	☐ 0
We have a formal process for following up with newcomers to the church.	☐ 5	☐ 4	☐ 3	☐ 2	☐ 1	☐ 0
I often talk to church newcomers who have had a positive experience of being welcomed at our church.	☐ 5	☐ 4	☐ 3	☐ 2	☐ 1	☐ 0
We are intentional and exert a significant amount of energy in helping individuals find a small group.	☐ 5	☐ 4	☐ 3	☐ 2	☐ 1	☐ 0
Our church has a clear understanding of the paths people take to become involved in our church's small groups.	☐ 5	☐ 4	☐ 3	☐ 2	☐ 1	☐ 0
Our paid staff and small group volunteers stay in contact with one another so that newcomers' needs can be met by the appropriate person or ministry.	☐ 5	☐ 4	☐ 3	☐ 2	☐ 1	☐ 0
When contacting newcomers, we make them aware of small groups that may address their needs and interests.	☐ 5	☐ 4	☐ 3	☐ 2	☐ 1	☐ 0
We have an effective system for managing the information we collect from newcomers.	☐ 5	☐ 4	☐ 3	☐ 2	☐ 1	☐ 0
We monitor our information collection system to ensure that we follow up and stay in contact with each visitor and/or newcomer.	☐ 5	☐ 4	☐ 3	☐ 2	☐ 1	☐ 0
When a person completely drops out of a small group or involvement in the life of the church, we know it and are intentional about finding out why the individual left.	☐ 5	☐ 4	☐ 3	☐ 2	☐ 1	☐ 0
When an individual leaves a small group, we attempt to place him or her into a group that better fits his or her current needs.	☐ 5	☐ 4	☐ 3	☐ 2	☐ 1	☐ 0
When following up with newcomers, we make an effort to connect them with someone who maintains personal contact as the individual connects with a small group in our church.	☐ 5	☐ 4	☐ 3	☐ 2	☐ 1	☐ 0
When providing newcomers the information they request, we follow up to ensure our response was sufficient.	☐ 5	☐ 4	☐ 3	☐ 2	☐ 1	☐ 0
When responding to newcomers, we communicate with the appropriate ministerial staff and volunteers so that everyone is aware of what actions have been taken to connect them.	☐ 5	☐ 4	☐ 3	☐ 2	☐ 1	☐ 0
Total of Each Score	___5s	___4s	___3s	___2s	___1s	___0s

Range of Group Experiences

Description	Evaluation Score					
Our church stays in tune with creative ideas other churches are implementing to form new groups.	☐ 5	☐ 4	☐ 3	☐ 2	☐ 1	☐ 0
Our small group ministry offers a broad range of groups appealing to different needs, levels of interest, and desires for intensity of study.	☐ 5	☐ 4	☐ 3	☐ 2	☐ 1	☐ 0
Seldom do our small groups become competitive with one another.	☐ 5	☐ 4	☐ 3	☐ 2	☐ 1	☐ 0
We have a variety of groups targeted to the needs of Christians at different levels of spiritual maturity.	☐ 5	☐ 4	☐ 3	☐ 2	☐ 1	☐ 0
We have task- or serving-oriented small groups that form to specifically meet a need of the congregation or the community we live in.	☐ 5	☐ 4	☐ 3	☐ 2	☐ 1	☐ 0
We have small groups for spiritual seekers who have shown interest in the gospel.	☐ 5	☐ 4	☐ 3	☐ 2	☐ 1	☐ 0
We work very hard to value all small groups equally, avoiding the tendency to see more mature Christians or groups as better.	☐ 5	☐ 4	☐ 3	☐ 2	☐ 1	☐ 0
When considering the creation of new groups, we look very carefully at unmet needs and/or interests of people.	☐ 5	☐ 4	☐ 3	☐ 2	☐ 1	☐ 0
When seeking new small group leaders, we look for those with expertise or passion for the needs of unconnected people (examples: new moms, empty nest parents, workplace leaders, etc.).	☐ 5	☐ 4	☐ 3	☐ 2	☐ 1	☐ 0
Total of Each Score	___5s	___4s	___3s	___2s	___1s	___0s

Multiplying Group Life						
Description	Evaluation Score					
Group members embrace the discomfort that sometimes happens when welcoming new members — seekers or Christians — and make an effort to create a warm, inviting atmosphere.	☐ 5	☐ 4	☐ 3	☐ 2	☐ 1	☐ 0
Small group leaders have been trained on how to invite people to groups.	☐ 5	☐ 4	☐ 3	☐ 2	☐ 1	☐ 0
Members of our small groups feel free to be themselves; they are willing to acknowledge their doubts and struggles.	☐ 5	☐ 4	☐ 3	☐ 2	☐ 1	☐ 0
New group members are always welcome in our existing small groups.	☐ 5	☐ 4	☐ 3	☐ 2	☐ 1	☐ 0
New group members are willing to ask questions, express doubts and fears, and tell the truth, whatever momentary discomfort it might create.	☐ 5	☐ 4	☐ 3	☐ 2	☐ 1	☐ 0
New members that attend our groups say they feel genuinely welcome or at home.	☐ 5	☐ 4	☐ 3	☐ 2	☐ 1	☐ 0
Our church frequently sponsors events and activities that appeal to a broad range of people in our community, which groups use to identify potential members.	☐ 5	☐ 4	☐ 3	☐ 2	☐ 1	☐ 0
Our church leadership (senior pastor, staff, elders, deacons, board members, and small group leaders) views our small group ministry as a key evangelistic tool.	☐ 5	☐ 4	☐ 3	☐ 2	☐ 1	☐ 0
Our group members do not assume that everyone attending a meeting knows how to use the Bible, and they are sensitive to helping people learn about it in a nonthreatening way.	☐ 5	☐ 4	☐ 3	☐ 2	☐ 1	☐ 0
Our small group leaders model openness to seekers and newcomers.	☐ 5	☐ 4	☐ 3	☐ 2	☐ 1	☐ 0
Our small groups believe they have an opportunity to have their groups share God's love and introduce individuals to a personal relationship with Jesus Christ.	☐ 5	☐ 4	☐ 3	☐ 2	☐ 1	☐ 0
Our small groups periodically conduct activities that encourage and welcome new members in nonthreatening ways.	☐ 5	☐ 4	☐ 3	☐ 2	☐ 1	☐ 0
Small group members are continuously on the lookout for new people to become a part of their small groups.	☐ 5	☐ 4	☐ 3	☐ 2	☐ 1	☐ 0
The leaders in our small group ministry are sensitive to the pain of feeling disconnected or isolated.	☐ 5	☐ 4	☐ 3	☐ 2	☐ 1	☐ 0
Our small groups that are usually closed to new members periodically open to intentionally welcome newcomers.	☐ 5	☐ 4	☐ 3	☐ 2	☐ 1	☐ 0
Total of Each Score	___5s	___4s	___3s	___2s	___1s	___0s

Open-Ended Narrative Questions

Description	Response
1. What do you think is the greatest strength of our small group ministry, and why?	
2. What do you think is the biggest challenge faced by our small group ministry, and why?	
3. Is there anything you can add that might help us to improve the effectiveness of our church's small group ministry?	

Totals from Each Category

For each category, transfer your total x's for each score onto the following table.

For example, if for Ministry Strategy your totals are 5 fives, 3 fours, 8 threes, 5 twos, 0 ones, and 0 zeros:

Total of Each Score _5_ 5s _3_ 4s _8_ 3s _5_ 2s _0_ 1s _0_ 0s

Then record those totals in the following table, do the multiplication, and then total those results in the final column, like this:

Ministry Strategy 5x5=_25_ 3x4=_12_ 8x3=_24_ 5x2=_10_ 0x1=_0_ 0x0=_0_ Total _71_

Category	Scores						Total
Ministry Strategy	___x5=___	___x4=___	___x3=___	___x2=___	___x1=___	___x0= 0	
Point Leadership	___x5=___	___x4=___	___x3=___	___x2=___	___x1=___	___x0= 0	
Support Structures	___x5=___	___x4=___	___x3=___	___x2=___	___x1=___	___x0= 0	
Leadership Development	___x5=___	___x4=___	___x3=___	___x2=___	___x1=___	___x0= 0	
Connection Strategies	___x5=___	___x4=___	___x3=___	___x2=___	___x1=___	___x0= 0	
Range of Group Experiences	___x5=___	___x4=___	___x3=___	___x2=___	___x1=___	___x0= 0	
Multiplying Group Life	___x5=___	___x4=___	___x3=___	___x2=___	___x1=___	___x0= 0	
Ministry Strategy	___x5=___	___x4=___	___x3=___	___x2=___	___x1=___	___x0= 0	

Weighted Average for Each Category

Insert the total category score for each category from the preceding table into the first column of the following table. Then divide the total category score by the total number of questions for the category, and record the result, which is a weighted average for the category, in the final column.

Ministry Strategy __71__ (total category score) ÷ 21 (total questions) = __3.4__

Ministry Strategy	____ (total category score) ÷ 21 (total questions) = ____
Point Leadership	____ (total category score) ÷ 12 (total questions) = ____
Support Structures	____ (total category score) ÷ 14 (total questions) = ____
Leadership Development	____ (total category score) ÷ 11 (total questions) = ____
Connection Strategies	____ (total category score) ÷ 14 (total questions) = ____
Range of Group Experiences	____ (total category score) ÷ 9 (total questions) = ____
Multiplying Group Life	____ (total category score) ÷ 15 (total questions) = ____

INTERPRETING YOUR CATEGORY SCORES AND AVERAGES

Once you have completed the Grouplife Assessment, compare each of the seven categories with each other to determine which is weakest. If you place them in order, from weakest to strongest (sometimes called "force ranking"), how do they stack up? List them in order here from the menu below, based on your "weighted average" conclusions from the prior page:

- Ministry Strategy
- Point Leadership
- Support Structures
- Leadership Development
- Connection Strategy
- Range of Group Experiences
- Multiplying Group Life

1.

2.

3.

4.

5.

6.

7.

Before you proceed, you can cross-check your findings by referencing the symptoms of weakness outlined below. Doing so will help you to validate your scoring and better understand the areas that scored lowest. It might cause you to make slight adjustments in the conclusions you have reached.

SYMPTOMS OF WEAKNESS BY CATEGORY

In Ministry Strategy

Leaders don't agree on the purpose of small groups.

Relationships are breaking down among those most committed to community.

Church members expect too much attention from the staff.

Small groups have a myopic vision and don't know their role in the overall church strategy.

In Point Leadership

The small group ministry does not have a designated, passionate leader.

An already busy staff member has been placed in charge of the small group ministry.

The church tries to have everyone do a little instead of having one leader lead.

The point leader lacks a clear job description and focused ministry objectives.

In Support Structures

The small group pastor is approaching burnout.

Spans of care are too large.

Coaches are unclear about their role and responsibilities.

Coaches are viewed as ministry channels, not as people.

In Leadership Development

Too many people have no identifiable shepherd.

Nobody knows the leadership development potential in the church.

There is little or no teaching about leadership roles and gifts.

Senior leaders are not modeling leadership development.

In Connection Strategy

Newcomers feel isolated and have difficulty finding their way to a group.

No system is in place for collecting data about newcomers.

No clear process or pathway exists to connect the unconnected.

No one follows up with people in the assimilation pipeline.

In Range of Group Experiences

There tends to be a "one size fits all" approach to group life.

Too few entry points into groups exist.

There are artificial limits on what counts as a small group.

Potential leaders are overlooked because of lack of group variety.

In Multiplying Group Life

No vision exists for filling open chairs in a group.

Leaders have not been taught how to invite people to the open chair.

Groups have little passion for seekers or fear having outsiders in their groups.

People don't know how to relate to lost people when they come to groups.

OPTIMIZING YOUR GROUPLIFE ASSESSMENT

The remainder of this chapter is intended for the point leader or core team that leads the ministry evaluation process. We have designed the content to serve two purposes: (1) to give you guidance on your own assessment of the ministry, and (2) to provide the assessment tool for easy recopying and distribution to everyone you want to involve in providing feedback on the small group ministry.

If you use the Grouplife Assessment as a periodic exercise for ministry review, it will serve you well. Expanding the circle of evaluators—for example, with a whole-church survey—can increase effectiveness even more. One of the best things a church can do is collect input from a wide range of individuals involved in the ministry.

Here are some of the benefits of engaging in a whole-church survey.

- *It refines thinking.* By gaining valuable input from a wide range of voices in the congregation, leaders sharpen their focus and avoid fuzzy thinking.
- *It minimizes blind spots.* We leaders sometimes only see what we are looking for, or what aligns with our personal vision. Consequently, we can ignore important data or perspectives that would enhance or impede progress. The more input we solicit, the fewer blind spots we will have.
- *It tests assumptions.* Data and feedback will always put our assumptions to the test. Our hypotheses and expectations must be challenged by reality.
- *It increases ownership.* The more contributors you have to the process, the more likely they will feel a sense of ownership of the outcome.
- *It builds trust.* When leaders operate in a vacuum, void of the contributions and input of other ministry stakeholders, skepticism and suspicion abound. People become wary of leaders who seem to operate secretly. Including and informing others keeps communication open and fosters trust.
- *It enables shared language to emerge.* By observing themes and trends in the data, leaders can choose language that will connect with a broader group of people. They can express ideas in clear, powerful words that will resonate with the church.
- *It brings honor to the community.* Since the church is a community— not just a team of leaders—the entire congregation can feel a sense of oneness as the mission is articulated and understood.

Doing such a survey requires increased work, to be sure, but the payoff is worth it. By collating every evaluator's input, you should receive significant perspective on the developmental progress of the ministry, and sharing the results should trigger productive discussion across your leadership corps.

Below we outline several points to consider when you increase the feedback pool. You will optimize the experience by leaning into the following recommendations as you engage your whole church in the assessment.

1. Don't Stop the Small Group Ministry

In fact, communicate that the assessment process is designed to improve everyone's commitment. Evaluation can reveal weaknesses, and therefore you do an evaluation as a kind of time-out before you make a next strategic move. One of the wonderful aspects of group life is that even when we don't get it all right, Jesus still shows up where two or three gather, and God will anoint any effort to unify and grow his bride-in-waiting.

Beware of the time it can take to prepare for and implement a survey process. It should not become the main task of the ministry. The tool provided in this chapter is designed to allow someone to complete it in as few as fifteen minutes. If they take longer, that is fine. The collective feedback is what matters most.

Tackling challenges in ministry is like changing a flat tire on a race car without taking it off the track. It would be nice to pull into the pit stop, but needs, care, growth, and leadership simply do not stop. This is all the more true when you intentionally seek feedback on how to improve the small group program in your church.

2. Involve Key Volunteers

This exercise requires a variety of spiritual gifts. You will need someone with the gift of helps to prepare material, an administrator to design good process, those with wisdom and discernment to evaluate the assessment, others with leadership gifts to strategize next steps, and teachers who can communicate results effectively. Gather a small, well-tailored team for this project.

Scan your congregation for a person or two who have professional training in surveying and interpreting information—someone who can supplement the paper assessment with focus groups to collect more input on your findings. The insight they will bring on how to assimilate the nuances without chasing red herrings, and about what is statistically significant versus misleading, will be of incredible value.

A dedicated team who can streamline the process will enable a quick turnaround. You cannot afford to have those you survey hear too late about something they participated in months ago. Prompt compilation and communication affirms involvement and will pay off the next time you assess (see recommendations 4 and 9).

3. Survey Leaders and Members at All Levels of the Church

Absolutely, positively include your senior pastor. Department leaders, key influencers, board members, and donors can also provide valuable perspective. Do not survey *only* those involved in small group leadership; but do include a healthy dose of their feedback—they should be the majority of respondents—since they will have the best vantage point on many of the statements the tool poses. Add in some group members and a few people who are unconnected to group life.

Keep track of where the responses come from. Anonymity breeds honesty, so group the audiences from which you seek participation, and then label the assessments submitted to that group so you can account for their point of view.

Expanding the circle of input in this manner communicates something about the church. If a church's aim is to increase an ever-deepening community, then breadth of opinion is mandated.

4. Celebrate Conversations as Much as Results

This effort is about the process, not the outcome. Depending on how you approach it (for example, see recommendation 10 on retreats), the discussions launched by the tool may produce more value than the data you collect.

Prepare for some chaos that might result from asking hard questions about group life. Your theology of community; the role of point leader, coaches, and leaders; and the purpose, focus, and outcomes of groups may come into question, but this will open pathways to alignment, leadership leverage, group expansion, and increased care and discipleship.

One of our mentors has given us a periodic reminder when we get stressed about the messiness of church work: you have to enjoy the journey more than the destination. There is always plenty to celebrate in ministry, but the work is never done, good enough never can be good enough, and we can always improve the ministry's fruitfulness. So finding the joy of engagement, rich discussion, and transformational efforts is the point. The outcomes will come in due course.

5. Feed Back the Feedback

Productive resolution of the conversations over your findings requires closure of the communication loop. Everyone you involve in the process needs to hear what you concluded during the season of reflection on the ministry in which they have a stake.

Plan when, where, and how you will do so, perhaps by audience, with varied levels of disclosure based on the nature of a stakeholder group. Your senior pastor and board members will deem fascinating some findings that small group leaders think inconsequential. One department needs to hear aspects that others do not.

Accordingly, segment the data by evaluator pool, as mentioned previously. Expect differences of opinion among various groups. As it makes sense, let people know what that divergence tells you. Convergence of perspective is helpful when you spot it too, and that is worth noting with everyone, especially as it leads to specific next steps to develop group life.

6. Mark the Pluses More Than the Minuses

An assessment can easily turn critical, especially one focused on diagnosing strengths and weaknesses. Negatives can become the size of beach balls while positives shrink to ping-pong balls. One benefit of community is that no matter what you find out, God brings good from it. The benefit of critiquing community is that we can then reshape it. There really are no bad outcomes.

Magnify all that is good early and often. The more public the forum, the more you will concentrate on the advantages, good news, favorable points, and instructive learning about community. Private settings will permit you to make your most incisive comments about how to define the deficits.

Although your conclusions should have a positive tone, beware of a couple of tendencies. First, spiritualizing can equal rationalizing failure of effort or outcome. You can spotlight God's good work while still projecting what has to be tackled. Second, you will find more than enough to critique—the nature of community is that it is fragile and its systems prone to breakdown—so learn what you can from the minuses and move on.

7. Prioritize Your Problems

Once you identify weaknesses, describe them well and include the right people in creating solutions. There will be too much to do. Assessing seven key categories will yield at least that many improvements. You will need to rank which ones you will tackle in which sequence.

This part of the exercise is like medical triage, when doctors decide what to repair and what to leave unattended. You can prioritize problems by letting everyone know what will remain in "the parking lot" (we have seen consultants legitimately include this in assessment reports). This will allow collection of eventual action or side issues without ignoring them.

Aim to narrow everyone's focus to the two weakest categories (as determined by the Grouplife Assessment's weighted average). Attacking the two biggest problems will inevitably lead to the most progress.

8. Focus Your Energy

It has been said, "You have done a wonderful job predicting rain. I need you to build an ark." Assessment surfaces problems; leaders solve them. By uncovering the challenges to overcome, you have defined your job in the coming months. Think of it as job security!

Solving problems involves determining who must do what, sequencing needed activity, putting timelines to action, and describing with specificity what a resolution will look like. We cannot overestimate the level of tenacity and vigilance required. Put concentrated energy against each issue, making each an opportunity, so that you do not waste the effort of small group leaders and participants.

Action may lead to resolution sooner than you think. When your team begins to see results, it will trip dominos of further energy. Every problem you solve will have ancillary benefits in areas you decided not to touch. If one solution has to lead another problem's resolution in sequence, it is essential to focus energy on priority issues.

9. Reassess Every Year or Two

If you take the measurement process seriously, share the results with the congregation well, and activate serious effort toward the challenges with highest payoff, it will produce ministry growth. Add the Spirit's anointing on your activities, some wise fine-tuning along the way, and ongoing learning via an embedded analytical framework, and you will see thrilling progress.

Soon enough it will be time to gauge the ministry all over again. One benefit of using the Grouplife Assessment with an expanded audience is that you have what analysts sometimes call "benchmarking" information. The first survey provides a baseline for future reassessment. Each subsequent analysis is then all the more meaningful for finding what your efforts produced and building a methodical approach to ongoing improvement to the ministry. As you add new leaders to the group life effort, their experience can be weaved into the past through the common assessment experience.

The recommendations described above apply all the more when you reassess. You may decide to retain only a portion of the full assessment or to alter the original assessment. No matter what you change, learning and growing the ministry will always be worthy of celebration and lead to progress, and it will help focus energy on the right problems.

10. Consider Using a Retreat

This final recommendation is a bit of an aside and applies across many of the prior ones. Having watched many churches try to use the information the Grouplife Assessment yields, we have found retreats to provide an opportune setting for gathering data, processing it, reporting it, and for strategic planning.

If you have an annual gathering that small group coaches and leaders, board members, ministry heads, and other senior volunteers and staff attend, you can use this setting to launch this invaluable fact-finding process. Large events can also be ideal on the other end of the assessment process, for reporting the discoveries and initiatives formulated from the assessment cycle.

As you repeat the exercise every year or two, a leadership community that becomes accustomed to self-examination, critique, and improvement will serve all the more diligently. They will find out regularly what a difference they are making and that their efforts are worthwhile.

THE TIMES CHANGE BUT NEEDS NEVER DO

One of the leadership stories from the early church that speaks volumes about how the church moved forward in power and effectiveness is found in Acts 6. Everyone loves Acts 2, which tells of Pentecost, the launch of the church, and a thriving new body. Or the Acts 4 story about Peter and John's courageous defense during early persecution or about how possessions were sold to help those in need. But Acts 6? We skip over it because it launches with the first problems in that first church.

The problems described in Acts 6 — similar to those Moses had to solve in Exodus 18 — have been with us ever since. Due to the increased size of the congregation, some were being left out, so their needs were not met. The result, one we face often in ministry, is that people complained. They highlighted the failures of the church leaders. To the apostles' credit, they responded immediately and created what might be dubbed the first strategic plan. The plan, which required the recruitment of new leaders and the building of systems to meet the needs, is described in five verses, but you can bet that it summarizes a sizeable management solution to a problem that might have derailed the church.

The results are similarly brief in description. "So the word of God spread. The number of disciples in Jerusalem increased rapidly" (Acts 6:7). Leaders listened, they responded, the problem was solved, and the constraint on growth was lifted.

Leaders of the local church continue to do the same thing two millennia later. What could happen if we simply organize the effort to find out what is holding our congregation back, and then rise to the occasion with strategic plans that work as well as that first one did?

LEADING CHANGE

Breaking through Barriers

We cannot provide an exhaustive tutorial on change management. It is a topic covered in depth by more gifted thinkers than us, such as Harvard professor John P. Kotter in his classic text *Leading Change*—which we recommend as a primary source for learning on the subject.

However, there are some aspects of leading change that are church specific, ones that supplement excellent material found elsewhere. Our comments come from the classroom we all love to hate, the school of hard knocks. We've led the transition process in congregations across the country and hope some of the sense it has knocked into us will serve you well.

Before moving to specific tools for bringing about change, and the key role vision plays in the process of change, remember the context for your work that we discussed in the introduction, "Change Is Possible." It is from this position that you lead the change process.

From this place in the organization you have the opportunity to drive change. Now, with some key tools in hand, clarity about how to discern the church's receptivity to the change, and some vision-casting strategies, you can begin the process.

FOUR INDISPENSABLE TOOLS FOR CHANGE

Although you must become savvy about managing change within the circles shown above, four unifying tools can help you along the way, guiding every audience through various aspects of the change process.

Books

A common set of ideas, transferable concepts and language, and fitting arguments for the ministry's direction are important when you guide a church into a new vision for community. If you can find one or two texts that best express what you hope to build, provide some insight into how it might look in your church, and create the conversations about transition, they can become crucial springboards to change.

A volume on small group models might be useful. A book on vision, along with a small group leader training handbook, could provide the needed education and inspiration. You may need a book for senior leaders, a different one for ministry department heads, and still another for those who eventually will be the seminal group leaders.

Blueprints

Just as a great architect can show someone what their new home will look like, those leading a small group ministry will need a blueprint of how the church could look if your dreams materialized. The redesigned church built on small groups can be touched and felt through this blueprint. Project the current growth rate, and assume that everyone belongs to a group and that leaders, coaches, and support teams are in place. Draw how the organization would look once all of it is built. Through this blueprint you can start to see the future.

Blueprinting your church can drive productive discussions about today, tomorrow, and the change in between. Role transitions, shifts in duties, ministry adaptations, resource implications, timing and sequence issues, and numerous other matters will surface as you diagram how the congregation could function through community. Without such architecture, ideas about transformation could remain only theory.

The Stop-Doing List

Legendary business author Jim Collins suggests that instead of a company driving change through another to-do list it should create a stop-doing list. The dirty little secret about most organizational change is that it usually requires the enterprise to discontinue existing activities if it really wants the new day to arrive. Not that anyone admits it. Instead, the focus is on what to start, not what to stop.

You cannot mount a fresh effort to build life-changing small groups without changing what the church is doing today. You may begin to come against sacred cows, misaligned efforts, and individual holdouts, but you nevertheless need to engage each circle in discussions about what must stop in order to actualize the new vision for community.

Key Influencers

You do not have to persuade every member of the church that group life is a good idea; but you need to convince a small fraction of key influencers, who will in turn bring everyone else along. The key is to figure out who those individuals are, where they are involved right now, and what they need to process in order to become walking billboards for the community movement.

Five to 10 percent of the people in your church act as influencers who everyone else will follow. Some of them are obvious, such as your senior pastor. Others are much more subtle, in that they could be a department head that will create early wins with new groups, a significant donor who will support with added resources, or a board member who pulls others toward fresh vision. Don't try to win everyone over, just the right ones.

You will find over time that mixing and matching these four tools with influential teams, departments, or strategic leaders will support your efforts to bring change. And the transformation will come over time. You cannot afford to be fooled by early progress, though.

DISTINGUISHING BETWEEN PHILOSOPHICAL AND PRACTICAL "BUY-IN"

Building a life-changing small group ministry requires three to ten years, and churches tend to declare victory too early. In his book on change, Professor Kotter warns of such a trap, an easy mistake to make when reorienting a church around community.

How do you avoid such an error? We have found it helpful to watch carefully the following sequence:

1. *Words.* People will start to speak using small group terms before they change their thinking about group life. Their ability to talk

community is good in some ways; they have to get used to the idea of something new and different. It does not, however, mean they have changed their mind about a different way of doing ministry.

2. *Thoughts.* Over time they will start to think differently about ministry, groups, leaders—but they still don't yet believe it. Having the key concepts in mind, including the essential vision, values, and strategies, shows progress. Moving from mere words to a full grasp of how a changed church could function does not yet indicate real ownership, though.

3. *Heart.* It takes time to build enthusiasm for the movement of group life. Each person needs to process out loud (words) so they can make sense of the new vision (thoughts). Once they assimilate it they can start to feel it; once they experiment with it, they will see how God moves through community. Watch for occasional passion and you will have seen heart.

4. *Behavior.* The ultimate destination is to alter people's behavior, so that community becomes an automatic reflex, the way people naturally do life and ministry. For example, when a church member lands in the hospital and she calls her small group leader instead of the visitation pastor, behavior has changed. When relationships become primary and the infrastructure fades into the background, celebrate heartily.

Many people talk about a "church *of* groups" but act like a "church *with* groups" (remember that distinction from chapter 1). Do not be fooled by what people say. You haven't reached the finish line yet. The win comes much later in the progression. You must make the most of new thoughts and tend them so they grow into a desire for community. As more and more people feel and act out group life, change moves from hope to experience.

Knowing the context of your work, and with an understanding of the tools and strategies described above, use the process time below to reflect on the existing level of buy-in to a proposed change. This will provide clarity about your current reality. For some of you it may look bleak, but do not despair. We have seen hundreds of examples of effective change and ministry progress. With God's abundant grace, a team of humble, truth-seeking leaders, and the will to persevere, leading change is possible!

PROCESS TIME 1

What Level of Buy-In Really Exists?

How embedded in our church culture is the small group vision? On a scale from 1–10, with 10 being highest, rank the level of practical (not just philosophical) buy-in for the following groups (remember: *buy-in* signifies the level of commitment or support a party has for a particular decision or change):

_____ Elders/board/governing leadership
_____ Senior pastor (including teacher and other primary "voices")
_____ Staff (paid and unpaid)
_____ Key influencers (5–10 percent of change leaders in your congregation)
_____ Small group coaches and leaders
_____ Congregation

PROCESS TIME 2

Where Do We See Current Buy-In?

What do we hear people saying?

How do our core members express their ideas about relational ministry?

continued on next page . . .

Where are people's hearts with regard to group life?

When have we seen automatic behaviors consistent with community?

PROCESS TIME 3

How Do We Increase Buy-In?

How do we increase the conversation about groups?

Where can we inform people's thoughts about small group ministry?

What will build enthusiasm for relational experiences?

Which ministry areas in the church best model replicable community?

THE ROLE OF THE PASTOR/POINT LEADER IN CHANGE

Knowing your role in the change process will eliminate much conflict and misunderstanding; and using the right tools will serve you strategically. But there is another essential aspect of leading change: communicating the vision.

Vision drives change, and without vision, change is impossible. Without vision there is no picture of a preferred future, no lofty ideal to which people can aspire. Without vision, hope dies.

It was a Spirit-empowered vision that inspired Nehemiah to rebuild the wall of Jerusalem in the midst of fierce opposition. The dream of an integrated, racially united America drove Dr. Martin Luther King Jr. to march on Washington, DC, energizing a new generation of advocates for justice and equality. A vision for serving the needy was forged when helping Civil War soldiers during a raging battle fueled the passion of Clara Barton to launch the American Red Cross—at the ripe young age of sixty.

Once you get vision it is hard to see anything else.

Not everyone sees the vision. Only a privileged few are afforded a picture of the future, one they now must steward and share with others. Others appear vision-impaired, incapable of seeing even in blurry relief what they can envision with such sparkling clarity.

What can we do if we have a vision—a God-given vision of biblical community for our church? How do we help others see what God has revealed in Scripture, shaped throughout the history of the church, and reenergized in your local congregation?

Casting Vision to the Vision Impaired

Despite the mystical and spiritual characteristics of many God-inspired visions, there are some very practical strategies for helping others see what God wants to birth in the church. Here are some ways to share a vision with others who have ears to hear and eyes to see. They are everywhere in your church; they just need some help from a spiritual optometrist.

1. Corporate Vision Casting (Catalytic)

Some people can cast clear and compelling visions when standing before large groups of people in a class, at a pulpit, or in a banquet hall. Their communication skills and intuitive sense enable them to craft words, phrases, and images that inspire others to see and embrace the vision. Their words are catalytic, inspiring hearts, informing minds, and calling people to sacrifice for the cause reflected in the vision.

Regardless of your oratory skill, as point leader you must be comfortable utilizing the large gathering for casting vision. If you are not the best speaker, choose a vision caster who understands the vision, preferably the senior pastor or teaching pastor. Leverage the abilities of a guest speaker to help the audience understand the vision and be moved emotionally toward action.

We have had the privilege of being such vision casters for churches, conferences, and leadership meetings where the vision for community can be articulated with stories and energy. It is a very exciting role for a church or a group life point leader to play.

2. Impromptu Vision Casting (Casual)

When the vision is fresh in your heart and mind, you are hard-pressed *not* to talk about it. Any vision worth embracing begins in the heart, is clarified in the mind, and then is expressed by the tongue. So when someone remarks, "I see we are talking more about small groups these days at church. Why are we moving in that direction?" you can answer with clear, inspiring words.

Impromptu does not mean "unprepared." You should have your "elevator speech" ready to give at any time. Picture yourself on the tenth floor of an office building and someone steps on the elevator with you. Before you descend those ten floors to the lobby, you'd better be able to answer if they ask, "Why does our church have small groups?"

At a coffee shop, in the church hallway after services, in a Sunday school class, or at dinner with some church families, look for opportunities to share some aspect of the community/group life vision for the church. Stories, anecdotes, comments about a sermon, or a well-crafted question can communicate your vision at the moment the opportunity arises.

3. Personal Vision Casting (Conversational)

A man spends the entire weekend at the small group vision retreat. You and other leaders pour out your hearts and share with the 150 attendees about the future of the church, the role of groups, and the opportunity for great impact ahead. The man hears four messages about relationships, groups, biblical community, and the role of shepherds in the church. The event is exciting and many people are energized and enthusiastic about the future. The worship is wonderful; prayers are prayed; people are encouraged.

On Monday afternoon you receive a call from the man. He asks about groups, community, the role of leaders—everything you discussed and answered at the weekend retreat less than two days ago. You wonder, "Was he even listening?" He asks for a quick meeting over some coffee.

On Tuesday you sit down with him and he again raises the questions and asks you to share the vision. It's awkward but you ask anyway. "Bob," you kindly say, "did you hear the messages this weekend? They were targeted at the very same questions you just asked me. Did we not make it clear at the retreat?"

You respect him, but cannot understand the disconnect.

He senses your frustration and then speaks from years of wisdom, decades of watching dreamers and visions come and go. "Yes, I was there ... and I heard what you all said. It was a great weekend." You think to yourself, *Okay, Bob. And your problem is what?*

Then he speaks the wise, discerning words you will never forget.

"I know what you said from the platform. But I wanted to see it in your eyes. I wanted to hear your heart, up close and personal. I wanted to know if you really meant what you said."

You sit quietly. You know he is not finished but you already feel like you just received a graduate school course in vision.

"I was at this church before you arrived." True.

"And, I will probably still be at this church when you leave." After more than twenty years this has also proven to be true for each of us, at least as formal, paid staff members!

"If this vision is from God, I am all for it. I will work and pray and lead to that end. And I will serve your team any way you ask. I just needed to know God was in this and that you believed this vision deep in your soul. And now I am convinced this is true. You have my commitment. Have a great day."

In that moment it was so clear. Some people—strategic, faithful, long-term servants of the King—need a personal, one-on-one vision casting experience. They need to "see it in your eyes" and know the vision is not hype or performance or a way to rally the troops to a program. They want to know if it is welling up deep inside you. They want to be convinced you have prayed and listened and learned.

The only way that can happen is through personal conversations in a restaurant or at a coffee shop or in a living room. It takes work, time, and energy. It might feel like hand-to-hand combat with some people, but it can be exactly what they need to jump into the fray and help build the dream. Often these people will become your best allies and fellow vision casters.

Key Components of an Inspiring Vision

Bill Hybels, who loves to share a vision more than just about anyone, identified two essential factors to consider when casting a vision. We have taken his teaching and created the grid on p. 203. Before we fill out the grid, let's describe the two key components.

1. Urgency: Why This Vision, and Why Do We Need It Now?

Some people think they are casting a vision but they are only giving an announcement. Announcements focus on information; a vision creates inspiration. Urgency conveys the sense that other commitments, opportunities, and preferences must be set aside to devote energy to the vision. Something that transcends us is at stake and it requires our full attention. It will have impact long after we are gone.

To convey urgency:

- *Connect the vision to Scripture.* We do not mean just throwing a few proof texts around. Make certain there is biblical and theological grounding to the vision, and show biblical examples of the vision.
- *Do "problem-casting" not just vision casting!* Like Nehemiah, who described the burned and broken wall of Jerusalem, help others see the problem (a lack of community, newcomers unconnected, hurting people not finding support, people not growing spiritually, unbelievers having no place to process truth and raise questions, etc.).
- *Show how the vision affects each person.* What happens to me or in my world if the vision is unfulfilled? What happens in our church or to the people living near our church if the vision remains dormant?
- *Explain why people must act now.* What will/will not happen today or this month or this year if the vision dies? People might see that the vision is important; but do they understand that it is urgent?

2. Call to Commitment

Urgency gets people excited and tells them why they need to act. But what exactly do you want them to do? Why do you need them? What role can they play?

The call to commitment must have the following:

- *It must be clear.* What specifically are we stepping up to accomplish? And don't tell me we are changing the world — that can be more hype than hope. Provide a clear description of the project or goal. Are we raising $10,000, starting thirty new groups, reaching twenty new families in our community, writing a groundbreaking training manual?
- *It must be doable.* When the point leader shares the vision, some may ask, "Can I do this? Maybe you can do this ... maybe she can ... but can I do it?" which means breaking projects or big visions into edible chunks everyone can chew and digest. "Next Saturday each of us is going to serve at the Howard Smith School in the inner city, painting classrooms, repairing plumbing and tutoring forty students in basic algebra. We need your help if you have gifts and experience in any of those areas."
- *It must accessible.* If I have to travel eighty miles on a workday to participate, I probably cannot. If the training is on Tuesday nights and that is my night for a board meeting with the local park district where I serve, then I cannot help. Do your best to make the commitment

accessible. If people's hearts want to serve they need a way to participate, so the ministry needs to be flexible.

- *It must be measureable.* How do we know when we have accomplished
  the vision? What does success look like? Help participants know that
  they have made a valuable contribution to the cause, which energizes
  them and helps them see how others are being served through the
  church.

Now let's complete the chart.

If you have a low sense of urgency and an unclear call to commitment,
then your vision is boring.

"Uh, we could use a few people someday, if you have some free time, to
help with some cleanup and repairs around the building, so let us know if
you might be interested."

This message does not convey a sense of need and does not seem important enough that anyone needs to do it—what ever "it" is—any time soon.
Your "vision" (or lack of it) underwhelms listeners and they are bored.

Low Urgency and Low Call to Commitment = *Bored*

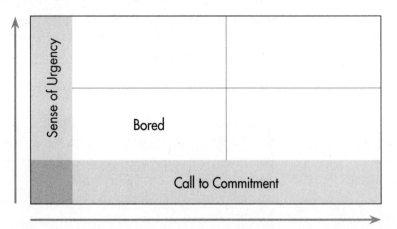

If your vision has sufficient energy and creates a sense of urgency, but
you are not clear about what people can do and how they fit into the picture, you create frustration.

"The gang problem in our city is on the rise, and it is starting to reach
into the suburbs! It could happen to you or affect your kids! We know that
God wants to reach these gang members and change their lives forever. If
that does not happen we are all going to suffer the consequences.

"What will the future look like for you and your family? What about
these students in gangs—they are throwing their lives away at such an early

age. We cannot just stand by and watch. Will you help? Will you stand with us to address this problem? How about a show of hands? Are you with me?"

This message alerts your listeners: the gangs are coming and God wants to change their lives, but what can any individual do? So they become frustrated.

High Urgency and Low Call to Commitment = *Frustrated*

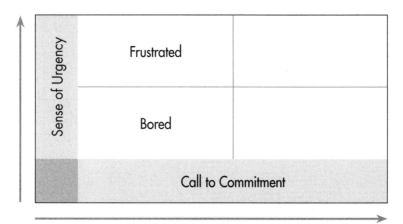

A low sense of urgency but a very clear call to action creates skepticism. Skeptical people might ask, why are leaders presenting all the specifics on *what* to do when we do not know *why* we need to do it now? Why waste the time and money? Are we sure this is necessary? Individuals who hear this become skeptical.

This "vision" is an example: "We want everyone in our church to be in a group, and there are plenty of groups to join. Don't worry about that. This month is group month and we are asking everyone to sign up for a three-week group experience in a home near where they live. The sign-up cards are being handed out now and you can drop them in the offering plate in a few minutes. Then you will receive a phone call telling you which group to attend, where it meets, what to bring, the day of the week, and the time of the meeting. All meetings will be ninety minutes so you can be home by 9:00 p.m. If you have any questions, call Karen at the church office. Okay? Great. This will be a wonderful experience for our church. Think of it … no one has to be without a group!"

Someone who hears this message would become skeptical and confused: Huh? Groups? Why are we doing groups? Will I know anyone there? What about my midweek class on Jesus? Are we doing these for just three weeks? How will this help me grow in Christ? I already have enough friends, so why should I go to a group? Now I am a bit skeptical about the whole thing. What if I get stuck with a weird group?

Low Urgency and High Call to Commitment = *Skeptical*

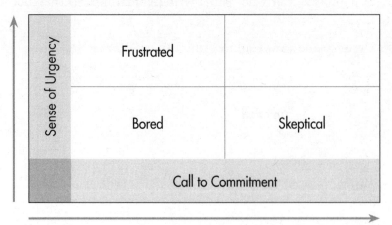

But when urgency is accompanied by a clear call to action, people become excited. They get enthusiastic about what the church is doing, why they are doing it, and how they can participate.

"There are forty thousand children in an area of Zambia who will not eat today. Nothing. Their families are displaced by war and famine; they have little shelter and no access to clean water. God's heart and our hearts break for these children and their families. Imagine sitting there watching your son or daughter die—and you know that just a little food or some clean water would change everything. God says, 'Defend the weak and the fatherless; uphold the cause of the poor and the oppressed' (Psalm 82:3).

"We might not be able to help all forty thousand kids—but we have estimated that if we each sacrifice and serve, we can help provide food and water for two thousand for a year. Two thousand lives change, and as we partner with ten other churches in the area, we believe we can help all forty thousand.

"You can help. First, we are doing a meal-packing day with one of our ministry partners. Details are in the handout you have. If we each volunteer two hours we will pack enough meals to reach the goal. Locations are in schools and care centers near your home—just refer to the list. Go online and register for the day and time that fits your schedule.

"Let's do this together. And then, the last Sunday of the month we are taking a special offering to put a well in the town. You will hear more about that next week. I am excited. If we all focus and do our part—if we each do a little—we can change a village! And won't that please our great God!"

When someone hears that kind of vision they can get *inspired*.

	Frustrated	Inspired
Sense of Urgency	Bored	Skeptical
	Call to Commitment	

Cast a compelling vision for community and group life that is clear, biblical, timely, doable, and accessible for your congregation! Cast the vision in newsletters, images, emails, messages, classes, and living rooms. Give it your best and watch what God will do!

PROCESS TIME

Improving Your Vision Casting

How well does your small group ministry utilize corporate, impromptu, and personal vision casting opportunities? Place each opportunity on the urgency/commitment grid based on the perspective of your church's senior/key leaders.

Now using the same grid, evaluate your own use of vision casting opportunities.

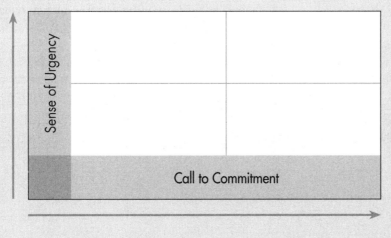

continued on next page . . .

What steps can you take to improve — both as a ministry and as an individual?

THE DOWN-AND-DIRTY DOZEN: TWELVE STREET-SMART PRINCIPLES OF CHANGE

Despite applying all you know about leading change, and the church-specific lessons outlined so far, transitions can become bogged down. Whenever you feel stuck with the change process, review this list of tenets on what will aid the gradual transformation of your community. It will not be a magic wand, but failing to follow one of these guidelines may be the weight that is slowing progress.

Principle	Why It Works
Love and respect the senior pastor and elders.	You will make more headway by loving senior leadership into change than by nagging. They are juggling more than your agenda. Esteem them and their roles, and they will regard your influence as worthwhile.
Teach philosophy, not just strategy.	*Why* matters more than *how* or *what*. People act on what they believe rather than what they ought to do. Change their values, and then their schedules, activities, and priorities will change.
Use consistent language.	Ideas are embodied in words. The small groups lexicon — such as an *open* chair not an *empty* one — will drive perspective, and embedded language creates ownership and belonging.
Use Scripture.	We've said it before, but it can't be repeated enough. The Bible is one of your best allies, not to manipulate, but because the God who *is* community can't stop talking about it.

Use stories that work.	Winsome pictures of life together create hunger, and a story lets people see a preferred future. Tell stories, interview leaders and members, and record videos so the essence of group life lives.
Use metaphors and analogies.	Whether family, body, army, plants, or a temple, the Bible repeats ninety-six versions of community imagery. We should too. Show people how relational all of life is, that community is the norm.
Use icons and symbols.	This is an endless well of vision. Batons depict the passing of legacy, keys the authority to lead, ropes the tie that binds, and so on. Give people reminders of the vision or value you've taught.
Expose competing visions.	When there is tension about where you are moving and when people resist, find out their alternative dream. Question, probe, empathize. Find out how their hopes differ from the vision.
Negativity motivates no one.	You cannot forbid renegade action, from prior ministries to active groups that won't align. It's okay. Don't make the past or people the enemy, or dishonor those who have made it happen.
Celebrate.	What you mark is what will matter. Rejoice often, in scheduled rhythms, and in moments no one expects. A party is sweet revenge for sacrifice, especially in community, for community.
Lead an evolution, not a revolution.	Leaders like a revolution. Followers prefer an evolution. The change you lead cannot feel like upheaval. It should be experienced as a timely progression toward an emerging future.
Never assume "everyone knows that now."	You've heard it: vision leaks. With group life, at times vision never stuck in the first place, needed another round to make sense, or got distracted by the urgent. Say it again. And again.

PROCESS TIME

Where Can You Put Your Street Smarts to Work?

Which two of the change principles above are you most consistently and effectively employing? Which two are you ignoring or underusing? Define one way you have effectively led change in the past six months and the specific ways you can put one of these guidelines in play within the next thirty days. If working with a team, share your perspectives on how these principles are working — or not — in your setting.

continued on next page . . .

Principle	When, How, and Where to Apply It
Love and respect the senior pastor and elders.	
Teach philosophy, not just strategy.	
Use consistent language.	
Use Scripture.	
Use stories that work.	
Use metaphors and analogies.	

Principle	When, How, and Where to Apply It
Use icons and symbols.	
Expose competing visions.	
Negativity motivates no one.	
Celebrate.	
Lead an evolution, not a revolution.	
Never assume "everyone knows that now."	

Chapter 10

STRATEGIC PLANNING

Key Questions for Data Gathering

KEY QUESTION

How do we develop a comprehensive strategy for building group life?

Strategic planning requires a clear process, a desire to achieve unity and clarity, and lots of work—which is why many people neglect it, shortcut the process, or simply pray and hope God will fix everything. After all, he is sovereign and will bring about his purposes anyway, right?

The Bible clearly states that wise planning is the responsibility of everyone who wants to succeed in life and work.

"Do not those who plot evil go astray? But those who *plan what is good* find love and faithfulness" (Proverbs 14:22, emphasis added).

"To human beings belong the *plans of the heart*, but from the LORD comes the proper answer of the tongue. People may think all their ways are pure, but motives are weighed by the LORD. Commit to the LORD whatever you do, and *he will establish your plans*" (Proverbs 16:1 – 3, emphasis added).

God is not against planning; he's against planning from wrong motives and planning that does not seek his guidance. James 4:13 – 15 says clearly, "Now listen, you who say, 'Today or tomorrow we will go to this or that city, spend a year there, carry on business and make money.' Why, you do not even know what will happen tomorrow. What is your life? You are a mist that appears for a little while and then vanishes. *Instead, you ought to say,* 'If it is the Lord's will, we will live and do this or that'" (emphasis added).

By thinking through a comprehensive strategy, leaders become aware of the potential costs and investments required for a thriving small group ministry. Given tight budgets and the responsibility of stewarding church funds with integrity, they must take time to plan. Plans do not master us; we control them. And planning does not mean you can never change direction; rather, a clear plan helps you recognize the need for change sooner, allowing you to alter course as new circumstances arise.

Referring to the cost of discipleship and of the commitment to follow him, Jesus said these words in Luke 14:31–33: "Or suppose a king is about to go to war against another king. Won't he first sit down and consider whether he is able with ten thousand men to oppose the one coming against him with twenty thousand? If he is not able, he will send a delegation while the other is still a long way off and will ask for terms of peace. In the same way, those of you who do not give up everything you have cannot be my disciples." What was true for Jesus' first followers remains true today: thoughtful planning and a firm commitment remain integral to their growth. And growing a life-changing small group ministry is no different.

Where do we start? Below you will find a series of questions to guide you through a disciplined process of investigation and data gathering. If you begin by faithfully working through these questions, you will set the context for developing a clear plan for building group life in the church.

EIGHT KEY QUESTIONS FOR FRAMING YOUR PLAN

Often churches eager to develop a new ministry focus primarily on the future—the vision, outcomes, staffing, budgeting, materials, and all the other resources necessary to get the job done. Before moving ahead to consider the kind of church you'd like to be, you ought to have a clear understanding of the kind of church you are. Here are some key questions to work through together as a team. This research will provide essential data for moving forward.

1. From where have we come? Trace your history to clarify your heritage, past values, attendance trends, and the stages through which your ministry has progressed over the years. Evaluate your history in light of some of these categories. Take about an hour, get in front of a flip chart or marker board, hand out some sheets of paper, and record the information for each of these areas.

- Teaching topics and themes
- Staff changes
- Major events in the church
- Major events in the world
- Changes in demographics
- Crises and tragedies
- Styles of ministry
- Financial challenges and major gifts
- Previous reactions to change

- Ministries started and ended
- Previous experience with group life

The exercise above will help you understand your identity as a church because it will provide a meaningful review of your past and allow you to learn from successes and failures and bring newer members up to speed with some of your more seasoned veterans. It also will allow you to celebrate what God has done so that you can begin to pray about what he will do in the future. Have older members tell stories about the phases your church has gone through. You will honor your past and create a greater sense of unity.

2. Where are we today? As an extension of the previous exercise, dialogue about present ministries, staff, vision, and effectiveness. What are you doing right now as a church, and how do you gauge your success in doing what God asks? What is your present structure or model for ministry (large worship gatherings, Sunday school, adult Bible fellowships, classes, small groups, informal groups, associations)? Why do you have each of these ministries? Are they effective?

3. What are our core values? Every church has a set of values by which it functions. Sometimes these are well understood and clearly articulated; in other churches, they are unwritten but understood by insiders. For a church to move ahead, you must first determine what values are central to your ministry. Only then can you determine whether small groups will reinforce those values.

Some values that merit discussion by your leaders are:

- *Building Relationships.* Caring about others and seeking to know and understand them.
- *Loving Lost People.* Since all people matter to God, lost people are close to his heart.
- *Truth-Telling.* Graciously and lovingly speaking truth to one another, not hiding issues, harboring resentments, spreading gossip, or avoiding healthy conflict.
- *Mutual Ministry.* Everyone shares together in ministry; it is not for just a few paid professionals. Honor the priesthood of all believers.
- *Accountability.* Committing to one another to practice integrity and moral discipline, allowing a brother or sister in Christ to inquire about each other's conduct and progress in carrying out responsibilities or behaviors.
- *Commitment.* Following through and owning responsibility for the mission.

Whatever you choose as core values for your church, be certain they are biblically based, well articulated, agreed upon by all senior leadership, taught, and modeled.

Now you can determine whether shaping a ministry around small groups will help you instill and uphold such values.

Take an hour and frame the top four or five core values that undergird group life, values that are consistent with the values of the church.

4. Who influences decisions in our church? Since this small group ministry is going to be a major initiative of your church, you want to make sure that most of your key decision influencers understand and embrace the vision, values, history, and current reality. In some cases, you will need their approval (elders, special committees, boards). In other cases, you will need their agreement (key volunteers, major donors, long-term members).

Caution: we are not talking about politics here. You do need to be wise about change, and the way it takes place. If certain people tend to influence decisions, direction, and strategy in your church, it is wise to communicate with them, respect them, and seek to gain their blessing on your efforts. You must go about this with absolute integrity and without manipulation.

Some of these people are not in formal positions of authority in the church, but may be married to people who are. Perhaps they helped start the church through their generosity and care deeply about its direction. Bring them into your process as counselors and advisers. Seek out their wisdom, listen to their concerns, give attention to the problems they raise, thank them for caring enough to work it through with you.

Realize that no matter what you do, some people just won't get on board. Be sure God is calling you and others to make the move to small groups, because if you are not sure, you will give up in the face of some disagreement or adversity. If it is the consensus of the senior leadership to move ahead, do so. Continue to love and communicate with those who will not support your efforts. Invite their critique. Continue to fulfill your God-given mission. Change always creates some level of conflict or disagreement. Expect it, prepare for it, pray through it, and move ahead wisely.

5. How will we craft and articulate the vision to our key leadership? Once you have consensus on the general direction and values, get a clear vision on paper. This will keep you focused and provide a tool for articulating your vision to those you lead. Include the biblical basis for your vision and values. Take your time crafting a compelling vision statement, and include many people's input. You want consensus from a large group of leaders so that as many people as possible "own" the vision.

As you go through this process, remember to consider what you want to avoid and what you want to preserve before addressing what you want to achieve. People feel safer talking about the future after you have assured them you want to keep worthwhile values from the past and are concerned about avoiding unnecessary problems in the future.

6. What are potential resources and possible barriers? What resources can help you to implement small groups? Below are some categories to consider, each of which may be a resource or a barrier depending on whether you have sufficient amounts of each.

- Leaders or potential leaders
- Finances—budgeted or outside donors
- Training and curriculum materials
- Audio-visual equipment for training and for presentations
- Staff—amount of time each staff member can devote to group development
- Consultants—experts from within the congregation and outside it
- A forum for dialogue and exchange—a regular place or meeting to evaluate results and handle difficulties
- Facilities for training and for meetings—off campus is best, but some groups will need to meet on-site

7. How should we repurpose or rearrange existing meetings to include group life? Depending on your existing schedule, you may want to leverage some meetings for training and vision casting. Many of your volunteer leaders and potential leaders are already committed to the church in various activities. Adding more training events and meetings to their schedules could overwhelm them.

Here are a few suggestions to help you:

1. Plan short training meetings before or after existing services. Ask childcare workers to work an extra twenty to thirty minutes one Sunday per month, and have small group leaders come for training during that time. Deliver very focused, specific training and communicate important information to your leaders without asking them to make another trip to church.
2. Change the focus of a Sunday evening or midweek service to accommodate small group issues and leadership topics. A sermon series could focus on any of the following topics:
   - Building lasting relationships
   - Truth-telling
   - Handling conflict

- Making fully devoted followers
- Using your gifts to impact others
- The "one anothers" of the New Testament
- Intercessory prayer

These topics will benefit the entire body, but leaders will be able to apply them directly in their groups. In essence, these meetings will provide a level of skill training. Provide a handout for leaders that can be used in their groups later that week.

3. Redesign some Sunday school classes around leadership training issues. Target a class for leaders of groups. Have leaders bring potential leaders to the class. Run the class as a "model group" as well as a teaching and training event. This kind of a class will have additional impact if the senior pastor or other key leader teaches it from time to time.

4. Add or include a group time or community-building time to existing board and committee meetings. This will help senior leadership model group life for the congregation, give them a taste of group life, and help them build a stronger team. As these men and women see the value of group life and how it can enhance their efforts, they will be more supportive of the church using groups as a means of doing ministry.

8. What are the implications for our senior leaders and staff? Initially, if a church is committed to having a churchwide group life ministry, each staff member will have to direct time and energy toward the development of groups and teams. This can be achieved by *growing* into small group ministry, not *going* into small group ministry.

Each year for three to five years, replace 20 percent of a staff member's job description with small group development responsibility. It looks like this:

Year 1: 80 percent current, 20 percent groups
Year 2: 60 percent current, 40 percent groups
Year 3: 40 percent current, 60 percent groups

This pattern allows a gradual move into small group emphasis by each staff member. It does, however, assume a few key factors:

- Twenty percent of current responsibilities must be dropped so that time can be spent building groups. In order for this to take place, you must help staff prioritize ministry responsibilities.
- Volunteers may have to be recruited to be part of the staff team. This is usually very healthy since many staff members view themselves as doers of ministry instead of releasing ministry to others.

- As small group involvement increases, staff will understand how mobilizing groups into areas of vital ministry actually helps get more done than if the staff member were doing it alone. Groups become a way of doing the ministry tasks that the church must accomplish while paying attention to the building of little communities where life change can occur.

LAUNCHING INTO YOUR STRATEGIC PLANNING PROCESS

Appendix 3 will guide you through an initial exercise to rank the subjects from strongest to weakest (this may match your Grouplife Assessment results), and then make room for discussion of the areas needing most attention. Once you have addressed the questions outlined above, you are ready to begin the strategic planning process using the work you completed during the "Process Time" segments contained in each chapter.

Remember what we've said before. You cannot work on all seven aspects of your ministry at once. Focus on the weakest or the highest-payoff two segments, then plan a handful of incremental steps in the next two areas, and formulate one or two key next steps in the remaining three.

Most churches benefit from planning on either a quarterly or ministry-year basis. Whichever you choose keep in mind that, as you enter into the final month of the current plan, you should assess progress and then engage in a similar exercise of setting the next round of priorities and activities.

Avoid the temptation to front-load all of your plans. Take all the allocated time and spread the work out over the entire three to nine months. Pay attention to sequencing, completing priority items first and then following up with secondary steps.

You will notice that each planning sheet includes a What, When, and Who column. Defining each is critical. Here is what each should have:

- *What*: Describe as specifically and measurably as possible the action(s) to be taken in order to make the desired progress.
- *When*: Put an end date to the action, realistic enough to be accomplished but sufficiently aggressive to inspire achievement.
- *Who*: Name the individual to whom you will hand the ball, and describe how they will communicate their progress with any team members.

What about those churches that are initiating a group life ministry from scratch or making a more substantive transition, repositioning the ministry? Phasing in the changes you plan requires added sensitivity and analysis as you plan. The last section of this chapter will provide you with an outline of how to phase in the ministry without shoving the change in people's faces.

Remember, the conversations and process matter as much as the outcome. Balance the drive to get closure on a plan with the need for adequate discussion. Knowing you will be back at the planning table from time to time will help bring the pieces together and provide you an actionable work process.

The benefit won't be just better groups or improved ministry. Every word on the pages you create has the potential to change a life, a family, a neighborhood, and a destiny. The planning will fulfill the highest of callings.

PHASING IN THE GROUP LIFE MINISTRY

If you are just starting groups or repositioning the ministry, here are some guidelines for steering the change toward a robust group life ministry throughout the church.

Many churches make a big mistake by diving into group life too quickly. Some ministries fail because churches decide to *go* into group life instead of *grow* into it. Pulpit announcements, launching too many groups too soon, not planning for success, and not allowing time for the training and development of future leaders can stifle attempts at developing groups. It is better to move in four phases, if possible.

1. The Modeling/Turbo Phase

In the first phase, church leaders (preferably including the senior pastor) lead one or two small groups. These groups should be filled with other potential leaders, people who have never experienced a vital small group, and a few people who have had less-than-desirable group experiences. Take the time necessary to model the vision and values you want for these groups. Experiment, take risks, invite feedback, and make changes. Along the way, you may have to break a few paradigms.

Each person has a different picture come to mind when they hear the words "small groups." Here are a few:

1. *Content-Intensive Bible Study.* Groups filled with informational discussions about Bible doctrines, interpretations of the second coming, and a focus on being right. Lots of notebooks, reference books, Greek studies, word study books, and other materials.

2. *Therapy Group.* Groups where people come just to discuss or fix their own problems. They typically have little interest in giving to others, studying the Word, or growing spiritually.
3. *Social Gathering.* Groups where people hang out together, have refreshments, share a few prayer requests, and plan the next event. This is not a bad thing because some of these more casual gatherings can create an environment for spiritual conversations and building relationships. Is this understanding of group life consistent with yours?
4. *Religious Discussion.* Groups where people debate lots of religious issues but never get at the truth of Scripture. Discussions focus on near-death experiences, angelic revelations, what all religions have in common, and the latest spiritual experience of a member.

These perceptions of what constitutes group life illustrate why modeling is so critical. Regardless of someone's background, they need to see exactly what you expect from a small group. Emphasize the distinctives your church wants to highlight. Show people how certain small group values are lived out as you

- invite newcomers
- train apprentice leaders
- reach out to seekers who don't know Christ
- prepare to launch new groups from your group
- handle conflict and struggles
- celebrate life change
- have fun
- bring creativity to meetings
- serve together

The very fact that you are in the process of developing a group will earn you the respect of others and the right to champion the vision.

An option to consider are turbo groups. Turbo groups (see chap. 7) are a strategic way for a church to phase groups in more quickly. At the end of a turbo group, everyone launches out to form their own groups. A turbo group allows participants to

- practice leadership skills
- begin the process of identifying their own apprentice(s)
- invite people to the group
- subgroup into groups of three to five for prayer and leadership development
- observe and practice healthy group dynamics

Turbo groups are great for speeding up the process of leadership development. But be careful—if this process is accelerated too quickly, you can turn these leaders loose unprepared. Remember, lots of future group members' lives are at stake. Taking time to train leaders sufficiently in the beginning will avoid a lot of problems down the road.

2. The Pilot Phase

With the pilot phase, all members know they are in a pilot group experience. You start by asking a handful of well-trained leaders to lead small groups for twelve to sixteen meetings. (It is good to do this many meetings so that groups get beyond the "honeymoon" stage and have some conflict.) After the final meeting, the groups pause for evaluation and feedback. Pilot groups still model and teach the core values you have decided upon, but they are not specifically designed to birth until feedback has been gathered.

The pilot phase is a great time to experiment. You have permission to fail because everyone knows it is a pilot and that they're going to have important impact in any changes that need to be made. During this phase you will want to meet very regularly with leaders. And leaders must be willing to push the groups a little. Because the number of meetings is limited, you want to make sure leaders use their time well.

3. The Start-Up Phase

Once a church has done some of the groundwork listed above, it's time to launch the small group ministry more broadly. This does not mean it is time to "go public." A premature announcement inviting everyone to join a small group is not a good idea. Not only will it create ministry chaos for the staff; it will cause you to put people into leadership prematurely and will frustrate members who try to get into groups but cannot find one that has room for them.

In the start-up phase you still operate mostly by word of mouth to advertise the small group ministry. Leaders and apprentices (having completed a turbo- or model-group experience) are now asked to recruit members to their groups. Each leader and apprentice team will recruit at least six people before beginning a group.

Before entering the start-up phase, make sure the leadership training process is firmly in place. Without this, you are setting leaders up for failure. Pay attention to these details:

1. *Location*. Where is the best place for a creative, dynamic training session?

2. *Time.* What is the best time for your leaders? Will you offer multiple sessions for them to choose from?

3. *Materials.* Don't give leaders poor quality materials to pass out. If you expect their best, give them your best. Use a good printer and copier, even if you have to do it somewhere other than the church.

4. *Duration.* This depends on how often leaders gather for training. If every six weeks, then take about two hours, provide a snack, and include huddle time with their coaches (overseers) or staff. If weekly, keep it to thirty to forty minutes.

5. *Senior Leadership.* Involve the pastor and elders often so that leaders know they are at the center of what's happening. Demonstrate that you value leaders by investing in them and providing them with current, up-to-date information about the church and ministry efforts.

6. *Coaches.* Begin to identify potential "leaders of the leaders" who will care for group leaders as your ministry grows. Don't overlook this, or you will have too many leaders under one person's span of care.

4. The "Going Public" Phase

If you have successfully completed the phases above and are preparing to develop coaches to invest in group leaders, then you are ready to go public with the ministry. Granted, many may already know about it. (Hopefully they have been hearing stories from pilot groups and small group leaders and can't wait to get into a group!) Before actually announcing that the church is now going into a small group ministry that encompasses the entire church, make sure you have considered these issues:

1. Are there enough open places in existing groups to accommodate new people?

2. Are you identifying coaches who will provide care and support to small group leaders? Staff and elders can initially serve as coaches, but ideally you want coaches to "come up through the system" after having led and birthed a group themselves.

3. Are you prepared to look for new leaders among those who express an interest in joining a group? Many good leaders are reluctant to come forward to lead. Be ready to challenge them.

4. Do you have a "holding area" ready if you are overwhelmed with requests for group life? These are classes where people can experience a small group format before actually joining a group. These classes allow you time to find more leaders and provide a place for those who are waiting to get into groups.

5. Are you prepared to pay the price? Your church will never be the same. There will be great challenges and issues to address (most of which are the products of success). Stay committed to the vision. Everyone in key positions of staff and volunteer leadership must be "on board" before you launch.
6. How will you mark and celebrate success? Storytelling is one of the most effective means to continue spreading your vision and strategy.

———

Be patient but intentional when phasing in a group life ministry. In doing so, you honor people and remain on mission as a community

EPILOGUE

End with the Beginning in Mind

At the beginning of this book we shared the story of First Community Church. Now that you have read it, their problems might not seem so formidable. Imagine that First Community had followed the process that you just completed. What if they had faced reality, set priorities, completed the rigorous work of evaluation and planning, and then pursued their emerging strategy with zeal and confidence? Their story—like yours—might be entirely different.

Four years ago FCC launched three new ministry efforts, including the redesign of a struggling small group ministry. Before diving in, however, the board and senior leaders met for prayer and began to diagnose the current situation. It was determined that the previous effort was thrown together hastily and had been an attempt to "close the back door" of the church.

To gain greater clarity, FCC engaged in a churchwide survey to understand the strengths and challenges of the existing groups, and to allow the congregation to provide valuable feedback. After reviewing the survey about the quality of existing groups, church leaders scheduled a full-day retreat for prayer and gaining clarity about the role and purpose of groups. The teaching pastor led several devotions and discussions using key passages about the nature of community life and the need for relational ministry.

In an effort to choose the right leader for the important role of heading the small group ministry, the church looked at existing staff, members of the congregation, and some outside candidates. Having gained clarity about the role of groups and their philosophy of ministry at the retreat, church leaders created a pastor of group life ministry profile. Each candidate was considered based on this ministry profile that was developed for the point leader position.

The budget for the coming ministry year did not include a group life position. However, the elders decided that funds originally assigned for two part-time roles (men's ministry and a pastoral counselor) could be combined for the new role. It was determined that the group life pastor could spend 70 percent of the time specifically focused on small groups and 30 percent on the strategy for the new men's ministry (which would largely be designed with small groups).

Finally, in order to communicate to the broader church the value of group life, each elder and senior staff member made a commitment to join or lead a group within the next ninety days. In addition, two teaching series were outlined for the coming year, and a small budget was set aside, by faith, to provide for leadership training and a small retreat.

FCC will assess progress every six months and continue to align ministries with the group life vision and values in mind.

Now that's a great story — defined by a clear mission, focused leadership, and intentional alignment with the churchwide strategy for making disciples!

Imagine a congregation that really believes in community and makes every effort to experience group life at the core of the church.

Imagine, as pastor Andy Stanley has exhorted, a church that is more interested in forming circles than in filling rows.

Community life is what we're created for and something for which every heart longs. It's what Christ desires for his bride, the church. And it is to this end we strive and pray and work by the power of his Spirit.

Jean Vanier provides a rich and compelling description of such a church, one filled with smaller communities gathering together as the body of Christ. It is with this kingdom picture of communal life we will leave you. May it remain fixed in your mind and alive in your heart.

A community is never there just for itself or for its own glory. It comes from something much greater and deeper: the heart of God yearning to bring humanity to fulfillment. A community is never an end in itself; it is but a sign pointing further and deeper, calling people to love: "Come and drink at the source which is flowing from the Eternal and which is manifested in each act of love in the community, in each moment of communion."

That is why communities must not be isolated one from another. They are called to live in communion and to collaborate with one another. They are all part of a vast body uniting heaven and earth, uniting those who have gone before and those who are present on the earth today. And together they are all preparing the seeds that will flower and bear fruit in the generations to come. They are preparing the ways of tomorrow so that the body of Christ may be fulfilled. Each community is but a sign of the liberating love of God. Some signify this love through contemplative presence and adoration, dwelling in the secret of Love, some through crying out words of truth, some through tenderness poured over broken bodies and hearts, giving life, reconciliation and peace.... This is the Church. (Jean Vanier, *Community and Growth* [Mahwah, N.J.: Paulist Press, 1989], 102–3)

"By this everyone will know that you are my disciples, if you love one another" (John 13:35).

READING THE BIBLE WITH AN EYE FOR COMMUNITY

Genesis 1:24–28. The creation narrative culminates with the paramount activity of God: the creation of a man. It is clear where he has chosen to focus his attention. The words that reflect his triune, communal nature—"us" and "our" in the Genesis conversation—are our words. We are designed in his image and reflect his oneness, the triunity of the first small group: Father, Son, and Spirit. At the dawn of creation he placed an eternal imprint of community in our souls. As a result we long for community with him, with others, for eternity.

Genesis 2:18–25. After granting mankind the capacity for community and the experience of oneness with the triune Godhead, God notes that man is not experiencing community on a human level. Man has no peer like each member of the Trinity has. Man is alone—and it is not good, not at all. So it requires one last, supreme creation—God forms a woman for Adam, and humanity is both marked and prepared for perpetual relationship. Loneliness remains the bane of existence to this day.

Genesis 6–9. A recurring dynamic in human society involves relational breakdown and redemption. Such brokenness is not limited to individuals; the entire community suffers and needs restoration. An early drama centers on Noah, God's handpicked agent for sustaining the race. When God becomes disgusted with the destruction wrought by man under the control of sin, he ponders ridding himself of the entire creation. But something intervenes—his unbounded love breaks through and is lavishly showered on righteous Noah. Through him our "expiration date" is extended, and God introduces a new kind of relationship—a covenant community—that becomes a central theme throughout the Bible to describe his relationship with the community he loves.

Genesis 15–17. When God makes a covenant with anyone, he marks them for himself (circumcision shows how seriously he takes it) and for the others who are part of the community he is building. In Abraham, God establishes a permanent bloodline that will produce the Savior of humanity. Through his recurring covenant action, God secures a group that will be the source of his companionship with people and their friendship with each other.

Exodus 18. Do you feel like bringing order out of community chaos never ends? It's not just your task. It has been going on for a few millennia, beginning with Moses and a post-slavery Israel. Exodus 18 is a case study in what it takes. Wise input (even from a father-in-law like Jethro), decisive action, leadership identification and deployment, and organization into groups together provide a template for inescapable community-in-disarray. Spans of care, sustainability of leaders, sharing the care load, and oversight structure remain just as important today.

Psalm 133. Community is described with poetic beauty in the Bible. When the psalmist praises the magnificence of human togetherness and unity, how does that compare to the "dew of Hermon" to be "falling on Mount Zion"? The rich metaphor says a mouthful, akin to declaring, "It is the best of earth touching the best of heaven." God adds his own blessing for good measure, just so we don't miss how much being together and unified matters to him.

Proverbs 15:22. The Wisdom Literature overflows with lessons about our divine design. Take our mistake-prone nature and a simple remedy for it. Decisions made alone tend to lead to failure. Input from others not only prevents simple mistakes people make; it inclines them to good choices and ultimate success. If you take an inventory of those facing adversity, you will find how often this principle is true. More often than not their trouble could have been avoided by a little counsel. People are designed to make key decisions *together*.

Proverbs 18:24. We are prone to approach relationships with contempt and ignorance. Treating people like products, we think the more relationships we have the better we will feel. Not so, God declares. In fact, it can be a ruinous path because it misses the point. Every person needs fewer but deeper relationships. Who has become like family? That is God's standard when it comes to the kind of community he's forging in the world.

Ecclesiastes 4:9–12. The quality of your friendships always surfaces in a crisis. When people find themselves in a ditch, the only way out is through others. At least that is God's point of view. So much so that he declares it pitiable to be in trouble without needed help. The implication: invest in community now, so you are ready for trouble later. The logic is overwhelming. If two are better than one, three are better than two, and so on. It is common sense that is not common enough.

Ezekiel 34. Community lenses make this prophet's words leap off the page. Ezekiel is charged by God to bring a warning, but not to the entire nation. Look at God's harsh words for those with shepherding responsibility. If you are a senior leader assigned the task of shepherding your parishioners and serving the community, take some time to reflect on this passage. The expectations are high, and God isn't ready to accept lame excuses for not getting the shepherding job done.

Mark 3:14. While crowds seek to draw Jesus out of solitude and into busyness, he decides to invest in a few. Rather than run with the pack, Jesus forms a little community so that "they might be with him." For most of us the applause and attention of the crowd would lure us to pursue a bigger and brighter life. Not Jesus. Instead, he pulls back and reins in a handful of men with whom to do life. A group to be with him, and he with them. In Mark 3 Christ makes a strategic and personal decision, a telling moment we ignore to our peril.

John 17. As his three-year itinerant ministry comes to an end, Jesus gathers his band of brothers and prays. He envisions an astonishing second phase of ministry his friends will soon discover and never forget. He earnestly asks his Father "that they may be one as we are one" (John 17:11, 22). Suddenly, the Trinity is no idle doctrine but a standard for group life, not just his group. He makes the identical request "for those who will believe"—you, and everyone you know—for trinitarian-level relationship. This stunning vision is an unending call for Christian community.

Acts 2:41–47; 4:32–37; 6:1–7. These are passages of contrast. The first two are snapshots of a burgeoning local church experiencing rapid growth. It thrives longer than most would. But the last scene shows what happens when reality hits. Expansion reintroduces a problem similar to Moses' Exodus 18 dilemma, when the load for too few leaders is too much. Not only do they suffer; so does everyone else. The solution? Organizational structure that ensures care through an expanded corps of leaders. The church has been in this grow-and-fix process ever since. It is likely why you obtained this book. You can see your future by looking at the church's past.

Romans 12. One of the frequent metaphors for community is a fully functioning body, with all parts working together for its health and protection. The focus is not on individuals and their particular gifts, as is often the teaching drawn from Romans 12. Yes, individual gifts are important; they simply are subordinate to the community—"each member belongs to all the others" (12:5). The result is love, devotion, honor, service, sharing, hospitality, blessing, mutuality, harmony, humility, and peace.

1 Corinthians 12. Perhaps Paul would have prospered as a stand-up comic. Have you heard his teaching on gifts in this letter to a notoriously dysfunctional congregation? His sly humor depicts a "gifts gone wild" church when put to self-serving use, exposing how facetious that would be. But it all leads to one conclusion, that each person is a part of his or her local church, and there has to be connection of each ... *each and every* ... part.

Ephesians 2, 4. In a flurry of metaphors about unity in the church, Paul imagines us all living up to being God's workmanship, heaven's citizens, God's household, his holy temple, and the Spirit's dwelling, all at once. That's just the beginning, though, since what he is really after is much greater: "attaining to the whole measure of the fullness of Christ" (4:13). How does it happen? Yet again, through an all-involved effort led by those devoted to building a fully functioning and unified church.

1 Peter 5:1–4. Now that you are seeing clearly through the lenses of community into the purposes of the church, Peter's description of the role of shepherd-leaders makes so much sense. They embody Christlike service, and he calls each of us to emulate them. Shepherding those under our care (willingly, eagerly, and humbly), we can expect a highly prized, eternal reward from Jesus ("the Chief Shepherd"). That will be something to behold.

POPULAR GROUP-MINISTRY MODELS

Cell Model (Ralph Neighbour, *Where Do We Go from Here?*)

- Evangelism is the focus; all life is in the cell
- Leadership development is key; larger gatherings of cells
- Website: *www.touchusa.org*
- Additional Voices/Authors: Randall Neighbour, Scott Boren

G-12 Model (Joel Comiskey, *Leadership Explosion*)

- G-12 (Groups of 12) are training groups; cells are used to find leaders
- Three groups per week, plus training, plus encounter weekends
- Website: *www.comiskey.org*
- Additional Voices/Authors: Larry Stockstill

House Church Model (Robert and Julia Banks, *The Church Comes Home*)

- Decentralization is key; leadership is cooperative
- Based on a family gathering, children included
- Website: *www.hccentral.com*

Free-Market Cells

- Short-term groups, driven by response to needs and interests
- Affinity is the organizing principle; leadership is fluid
- Website: *www.newlifechurch.org/smallgroups*

Metachurch (Carl George, *The Coming Church Revolution*)

- Leadership development through apprenticing
- Promotes open chair and birthing; intentional discipleship
- Website: *www.metachurch.com*

Sermon-Based Groups (Larry Osborne, *Sticky Church*)
- Groups use studies based on sermons each week
- Structure similar to metachurch or purpose-driven
- Website: *www.stickyteams.org*

Adult Bible Fellowships (Knute Larson, *The ABF Book*)
- Small groups formed out of ABFs
- ABF is primary place for building community
- Website: *www.abfresources.com*

Purpose-Driven Small Groups (Steve Gladen, *Small Groups with Purpose*)
- Groups led by hosts
- Groups mostly use DVD-curriculum in six-week series
- Churchwide campaigns are main catalyst for starting new groups
- Website: *www.saddlebackresources.com*

Common Cause (Robert Lewis, *Church of Irresistible Influence*)
- Small groups initially formed for fellowship—up to three years
- Groups then take on a cause in the community
- Website: *www.fbclr.com*

CHECKLIST FOR EVALUATING SMALL GROUP MODELS

After you have worked through this material, use this list to assess small group models you read about, or that you see others using.

1. **Ministry Strategy**
   - *Biblical Support.* How is Scripture used to create a theology for small groups in the local church?
   - *Vision for the Church.* What view does the model have of the local church and how are small groups integrated into the overall philosophy and strategy?
2. **Point Leader**
   - *Role of Senior Leadership.* How supportive of the point leader are the senior pastor, elders, deacons, or other key boards and committees?
3. **Support Structure**
   - *Organization and Structure.* What is the span of care that is provided and how does the structure release people for ministry?

- *Supervision Process.* What role do staff and coaches play in the supervision of small group leaders, and how are people held accountable for results?

4. Leadership Development

- *Leadership Development.* How are existing leaders supported and developed and what is the strategy for developing apprentice leaders?
- *Evaluation and Feedback Process.* How often is evaluation provided to leaders in the small group structure and what criteria are used for measuring success?

5. Connection Strategy

- *Assimilation Pathway.* How does someone move from visitor to being fully connected in a small group, and who is responsible for this?

6. Group Variety

- *Definition of Discipleship.* What does a disciple look like in your church?
- *Intensity Levels.* Are there a variety of group experiences for all levels of spiritual maturity and participation?

7. Open Groups

- *Meeting Format and Frequency.* How often should groups meet, and what is accomplished when they gather?
- *Use of Curriculum.* How is small group curriculum used, and who is responsible for selecting or developing study guides?

STRATEGIC PLANNING GRID AND WORK PAGES

As you finish working through this book as a team, you will have a great deal of material to process. To sift through all of it and begin to move forward, you need to prioritize the issues. Then you can begin to develop a plan. Use the material that follows to guide the process.

First, prioritize the major strategic areas your church has been addressing. What needs attention first, and why? Refer back to your notes and then rank the areas below on a scale of 1 to 7 with 1 being the highest priority.

____ Clarity on Strategic Direction
____ Establishing and Empowering a Point Leader
____ Implementing a Workable Support Structure
____ Promoting Leadership Development
____ Creating a Connection Strategy
____ Expanding the Small Group Ministry
____ Multiplying Groups and Leaders

Second, once you have prioritized the issues, go back to the process times from each section. Summarize and bring that material into the following charts. Begin with your number one priority and work through the process.

Strategic Planning Grid

Priority 1_____

Begin to put action steps to the work by using the chart below.

- *What* steps will your team commit to making in the next twelve months?
- *When* will you begin/complete these steps?
- *Who* will have primary responsibility for this task?

What	When	Who

Strategic Planning Grid

Priority 2_____

Begin to put action steps to the work by using the chart below.

- *What* steps will your team commit to making in the next twelve months?
- *When* will you begin/complete these steps?
- *Who* will have primary responsibility for this task?

What	When	Who

Strategic Planning Grid

Priority 3_____

Begin to put action steps to the work by using the chart below.

- *What* steps will your team commit to making in the next twelve months?
- *When* will you begin/complete these steps?
- *Who* will have primary responsibility for this task?

What	When	Who

Strategic Planning Grid

Priority 4_____

Begin to put action steps to the work by using the chart below.

- *What* steps will your team commit to making in the next twelve months?
- *When* will you begin/complete these steps?
- *Who* will have primary responsibility for this task?

What	When	Who

Strategic Planning Grid

Priority 5_____

Begin to put action steps to the work by using the chart below.

- *What* steps will your team commit to making in the next twelve months?
- *When* will you begin/complete these steps?
- *Who* will have primary responsibility for this task?

What	When	Who

Strategic Planning Grid

Priority 6_____

Begin to put action steps to the work by using the chart below.

- *What* steps will your team commit to making in the next twelve months?
- *When* will you begin/complete these steps?
- *Who* will have primary responsibility for this task?

What	When	Who

Strategic Planning Grid

Priority 7_____

Begin to put action steps to the work by using the chart below.

- *What* steps will your team commit to making in the next twelve months?
- *When* will you begin/complete these steps?
- *Who* will have primary responsibility for this task?

What	When	Who